A Very
# BRADY
Guide to Life

# A Very
# **BRADY**
# Guide to Life

## Groovy Solutions to Life's Most Puzzling Dilemmas

# Jennifer Briggs

**Rutledge Hill Press**
*Nashville, Tennessee*

Published in Nashville, Tennessee, by Rutledge Hill Press, 211 Seventh Avenue North, Nashville, Tennessee 37219.
Distributed in Canada by H. B. Fenn & Company, Ltd., 34 Nixon Road, Bolton, Ontario L7E 1W2.
Distributed in Australia by Millennium Books, 33 Maddox Street, Alexandria NSW 2015.
Distributed in New Zealand by Tandem Press, 2 Rugby Road, Birkenhead, Auckland 10.
Distributed in the United Kingdom by Verulam Publishing, Ltd., 152a Park Street Lane, Park Street, St. Albans, Hertfordshire AL2 2AU.

Typography by Roger A. DeLiso, Nashville, Tennessee

Design by Harriette Bateman

**Library of Congress Cataloging-in-Publication Data**
Briggs, Jennifer, 1961 Jan. 23–
    A very Brady guide to life : groovy solutions to life's most
puzzling dilemmas / Jennifer Briggs.
        p.    cm.
    ISBN 1-55853-447-4 (pbk.)
    1. Brady bunch (Television program)—Miscellanea.   2. American wit
and humor.   I. Title.
PN1992.77.B733B75  1996
791.45'72—dc20                                              96-22303
                                                            CIP

Printed in the United States of America

2  3  4  5  6  7  8  9—99  98  97  96

*For my parents, Momma and Daddy*

*For my god, God*

*For my bestest pal, Joseph Richard*

# Contents

# Acknowledgments

In a very non-Brady, disorganized order, I wish to express thanks to my oldest bestest friend, Doug Hudson; and to my best girlfriend ever, June Naylor, because I missed her birthday at the beach while writing this and maybe this book will be as cool as when she won the State Fair corn bread cook-off.

Also, thanks to . . .

My sister, Jan McDaniel, whose habitual successes gave me true empathy for Jan Brady.

Mike Towle, my editor, who is a real nice guy, and that other guy, Larry (Stone), who works with him.

A special thanks to Rhonda McNew, Doug Bradham, Debbie Foster, Brack Bledsoe, Tina Ward, Linda Denson, Lisa Gabrielle, Joey Funke, Amy Lloyd, Revo, Jim Brady, and Kristen Kaski (who does the best Jan imitation ever), who all helped on this more than they realized.

Another special thanks to Howard, Stuart, and Ethan

McDaniel, Bud, Opal, Hazel, Harriett, A. D., Claude, Louise, Tootie, Ronnie, Alan, David, Denny, Carl, Carol, Patty, Zelma, Albert, Minnie, Ardie, Margie, Pam, Butch, Frankie, James, Karen, Angela, Rachael, and Anna.

And my special friend, J. C., who makes all my best work possible.

Dr. Emilio Bombay for his computer prowess on this effort.

The Pabst Brewing Company for its valued assistance.

The prayers of Anne, Nina, and Mike, Phil, and Jeff (who really counts extra because he is a priest).

That guy at the Quickie Mart who asked if I was in town with Clint Black, thus providing that gee-you-kinda-look-like-Lisa Hartman adrenaline high the day this thing got finished. (Then followed with "but your butt's a little bigger," thus providing that Jan Brady-like manic-depressive low.)

Andrew J. Edelstein and Frank Lovece, who wrote *The Brady Bunch Book*; Elizabeth Moran, who did *Bradymania*; and Anthony Rubino, who did *Life Lessons from the Bradys*; plus, those guys who had Brady pages on the Internet.

And finally (Wow! I'm out of breath like I've just done

a potato sack race on Astroturf), thanks to Joe Rick Kaski, who watched eight Brady episodes back-to-back with me after driving my nephew and seven other seniors to the prom in an eight-door, green Checker taxi. Joe Rick is my newer bestest friend than Doug Hudson, and he does a real good job at it despite his lack of experience. He did a lot of mixing of computer diskettes and files and stuff that I can really screw up without trying. He also fed me and doctored my hurt knee, and he stayed calm when I acted like that really bitchy girl on *Melrose Place*. He did copyediting for me and also a lot of laundry while I was on deadline. All this on Alice's wages.

Rick, who is kinda okay for a cheesehead, knows it's easy to like a creative person, but a lot harder to love them. He hangs around anyhow and makes me better and less-Jan-Brady-like almost every day. Thanks to Rick, I may never rob a liquor store (though the Macy's is still a question mark). And plus, he's a real dreamy bo-hunk.

# Introduction

**W**hy *A Very Brady Guide to Life?* When as kids we spent the night, we hardly ever watched the Bradys on TV on Friday nights, to tell the truth. Instead, we did stuff that was probably a lot like what the Brady kids would do.

During the winter, girlfriends and cousins stayed over, and we did stuff like crank-call the teachers and write letters to *16* magazine asking them to please forward the enclosed love note to Davy Jones. Or sometimes I'd write Peter Tork because the dorkiest Monkee seemed like a more realistic goal since my hair didn't move all at once when I walked like it did for Marcia or even Jan.

In the summer, like the Bradys might have, we played outside late and ran races in the grass—except ours was real, and my mom was always griping about how if she didn't mow that Saint Augustine, it would never get done. But more often than not, somebody was grounded or somebody ticked off their parents by having the wrong attitude while asking to spend the night with someone and we ended up alone at home with our very hands-down favorite TV show for company. It's true. Check my diary, or Lisa Greene's or Haley Farr's or Amy Western's.

We lived and died waiting for the 3:30 P.M. winter Friday school bell that meant the Bradys were just a few afternoon reruns and a Banquet TV dinner or chicken pot pie away. Like a supermodel snapshot for a dateless guy, Brady life was just vaguely attainable enough in fantasy to make the weekly escape palpable.

My dad didn't get home at 3:00 P.M. like Mike. He fought traffic from the suburbs to Dallas and back every day. My sister is eleven years older than me, and there weren't any kids I could play with in the neighborhood, except when the people across the street's niece and nephew came over from Dallas, but she was hateful and once stole one of my dolls.

I always wanted brothers and sisters—at least enough to have some kind of sports team or to look out for me at school when Jace Hinkle and Kevin Stone made fun of the way I ran pigeon-toed. More than that, I always wanted our house to have an upstairs and a staircase just like that one on the Bradys with the rocks and ferns and open-underneath-thing going on. Maybe you did, too. Why *A Very Brady Guide to Life?* That's why.

The year the television Bradys were born and in the ensuing four years, the single gene was isolated—as Jan sank further into her middle-child isolation. Real-world developments opposite Bradymania offered other interesting contrasts:

- The Department of Health banned the use of cyclamates (an artificial sweetener), while Alice cooked blissfully along with full-octane pure cane.

- Dr. Spock's draft evasion conviction was overturned, while the aforementioned maid was turning over pancakes for eight (since she never ate).

- Walter Cronkite had the Chicago Seven. Sherwood Schwartz had the Clinton Way nine (counting the maid).

- Nixon said recent secret U.S. peace proposals had been rejected, while Marcia was rejecting hunk-o-rama Doug Simpson.

- Nixon was calling for a guaranteed minimum income, while Carol was calling the stragglers to breakfast.

- United States and South Vietnamese troops captured Hamburger Hill, and Sam the Butcher handed over ground beef in twenty-pound increments.

- America's back was against the wall in Vietnam, but no one's back was ever to the camera at the breakfast table in Alice's breakfast nook.

- The first women FBI agents were sworn in, but it was still boys are better than girls at camping.

That's why *A Very Brady Guide to Life*.

Yes, the Brady life was ludicrous. But so is *Baywatch* and so was Rose Marie getting career CPR on *Hollywood Squares*. At least the Bradys always had a small problem and a resolution with a moral before *Love, American Style* came along and we had to turn the channel or go to bed because they got too nasty on there.

The Bradys were just believable enough to be a believable respite. Oh sure, we all knew the frustration of not being like them. It certainly caused me and my friends our share of angst: we could never be quite like those three very lovely girls. Here I was, shaking the hand of *Gunsmoke's* Festus at Fort Worth's Southwestern Exposition Fat Stock Show and Rodeo, while Marcia got to snag Davy Jones for the prom. Life isn't always fair.

I won a Mountain Dew slogan contest during my elementary school years, while the Bradys won variety shows and Marcia, forgodsakes, won everything but hair transplants and Henry Kissinger's affections. That's why *A Very Brady Guide to Life*.

Wouldn't it be great if, just for a little bit now and then, life was like it was in that household? If Mike would have shut up now and then it would have been perfect. They lived in a big house with shared hair bows, and the grandparents and aunts and uncles didn't die because you never saw them. Tiger didn't dig out and get hit by a car, either. Then again, we didn't see a whole lot of Tiger, did we?

Think about it. If we all followed the Bradys' lives, stuff would be a lot different. Now, this ain't to say there would be cold fusion by now and Reagan would have stayed in California and Davy Jones would have gotten down on one knee in Shakey's Pizza and asked me to play his tambourine forever. But what if we'd all done like Marcia and spurned Doug Simpson for the nerdier guy, appreciating the inner qualities of a man? Wouldn't a lot of us still be married because we picked better the first time? I know I wouldn't still be paying off seven-year-old Visa bills.

What if we respected our spouses like Carol and Mike did and offered consistent (though nerdy) discipline to our kids like they did? This little mall monkey wouldn't have been breaking into my Jeep last week and my mee-maw wouldn't have gotten her lawnmower stolen in 1978.

We'd all be better following the Bradys' example.

And still, we gotta wonder if Carol Brady ever wanted Shirley Jones's family, or if Marcia had a secret and evil envy of Jan's tan. Did Mike Brady have a dark side that went from bar to bar trying to impress trashy women by telling them he taught I. M. Pei everything he knows? Did Greg flail away at that bogus Johnny Bravo singing career, unable to deal with his lack of stardom, and eventually end up relegated to performing warm-up for Shogi in Branson, Missouri?

"About fifty times," was our sarcastic phrase for the word "no" when in elementary school. Then again, if I brushed my hair one hundred times each night like Marcia, I'd have some really gross-out-lookin' split ends.

The Bradys were an escape because they lived in total isolation—a vacuum where the bigger pains in the butt like Vietnam and Nixon were basically ignored. Consider that when turning these pages, because we've got the Bradys now dealing with some topics and issues they never even considered until now.

This book is the compilation of the best advice-seeking letters sent to each of the Bradys, Alice, and even Sam the Butcher, accompanied by their respective—and respectful—responses which, although dictated by each character, are presented here in written form—constituting their '70s-type advice for '90s-type problems. For good measure, various lists of dos, don'ts, bests, and worsts have been added to further illustrate the Brady take on life. However, it can't be said that they have ever dealt with anything particularly well, except perhaps potato sack races and hair conditioning.

They *are* Bradys, after all.

And, after careful Ouija board consultation in Lucy Ricardo's living room, a trip back in time was required to nail down a few important subjects never broached by the Bradys. You know, things such as Bobby's favorite candy or the fact that they were actually TV characters on a TV studio set and their lawn was made of Astroturf.

And even when we were kids, didn't you think it just a little bit weird that Carol changed clothes something like three or four times a day and wore more in bed than she did at any other time of day, including time spent in variety shows? Mike could not have been diggin' this.

**Gosh darn it—isn't it fun being a Brady?**

# A Very
# **BRADY**
# Guide to Life

# THE BRADYS'
# Ten Answers for Gettin' Along in the World

1. Find what you do best and do your best with it.

2. If Davy Jones says, "How 'bout the flip side?" that means to kiss his other cheek.

3. If the receptionist from *The Bob Newhart Show* sells you a wig, it might look better.

4. Pull one little piece of hair back from each side of your forehead and put each in a barrette on the sides of your head.

5. The oldest brother should never, ever look at his sister's pelvis like that.

6. Get a marketing contract with a big automaker and you'll get to drive away from the house in one Chrysler and come back in another.

7. If the receptionist from *Bob Newhart* is your teacher, she probably won't get it when you tell her Davy Jones really isn't coming to the prom.

8. If the whole family and the maid paint the parents' bedroom, it means you'll never get divorced or fat, but the room will be really blue and Dad's hair will eventually get really curly.

9. If the receptionist from *Bob Newhart* is the voice of the receptionist at the hotel where Davy Jones is staying, you'll probably have better luck getting through on *Newhart*.

10. Ignore stuff like moon landings and Nixon because they'll only get in the way of potato sack races.

# I Am **Carol**,
# Hear Me Roar

**(Or, how to get your maid to work for
free and still have time for losing your
individuality in your spouse)**

**K**eep your guy happy, that's all I can say. Always allow time for your pursuits that give your life meaning. After all, maybe he has a career, but can your guy stitch an eagle on a dining-table-chair cover?

Can your guy fit into a size-eight, knit, bell-bottomed jumpsuit? Of course not. Can your guy—oops, or I guess I should say, would your man, take his maid shopping? There ya go.

But hey, always support your guy. Listen up. His advice is usually best. Tilt that head and control that posture when he's on the phone, even if you are just dying to hear about his latest success.

Sitting in the den is usually best—well, his lap is better, but when the kids are concerned, sit tight in that den by the backyard so you can be sure to catch the kids going in and out. Use that time to do your needlepoint or take the kids' phone calls.

This is also a good time to hedge off all but the toughest problems before they reach the den and consequently reach the man who has other things on his mind.

You don't really have to cook a lot, but PTA work is necessary for keeping a handle on what really matters most in life—your guy and your kiddos.

But enough about me. Let's get to the mailbag.

Dear Carol,
   My husband and I are raising five kids and it has been a struggle, especially since my husband Parley got laid off by the General Motors. We are four months behind in the mortgage on the trailer we started saving for when he got his GED, and me, my high school diploma. He can't find no more work, anyway, on account of he's been kind of sick since he got back from the Persian Gulf.

I was wondering if you could help me figure out a way to make our dollar go further, feed all these kids, and save our trailer on one income (I wash hair at the Shear Delights).

Plus, one of our boys, Duncan, won't go to school. We think he's in trouble and he hangs out in the backyard all day just smoking cigarettes and beating on the trash-can lid like a nut.

Help soon, or we may have to go to a shelter.

Thank you for your help,
Jan McDaniel
Arlington, Texas

Dear Jan,

Why, Jan, your family is large enough to put on a whole variety show. On a limited budget, costumes can be a problem, but if your maid is like ours—handy with the ol' needle and thread and works for free—she can probably whip you guys up a suitable wardrobe in a jiffy.

The money you raise from the show can go toward your house payments, although more than likely you'll get a huge recording contract and will be working at the studio before you know it.

Don't have any music or choreography worked up just yet? Hey, not to worry, Jan. It sounds to me like Duncan has already been thinking about his ol' mom and dad and been practicing on some makeshift drums to get ready for a fund-raiser.

If your husband is like my Mike and hits a grand slam each time he goes to bat with his architectural firm, he could probably also remodel your home and resell it for four times the price you paid for it.

As for food and economy, we find that making meat loaf in twenty-pound portions really helps economize on time. And always fry in Wesson oil!

And hey—just remember that whatever happens, as my Mike says, "Your home, and you, is wherever you are." (Oh, that guy!)

And keep those lines of communication open. Always talk together with your guy, even if it's late at night, and you're a bit on the tired side having just finished another needlepoint and he's probably pooped from another chapter of *Jonathan Livingston Seagull*.

Best of luck,
**Carol Brady**

Hey, see what I mean, here? If you can sew and sing, the possibilities are endless.

## Brady Tips for Shopping for Stuff

1. Get a car that's the same avocado green as your washing machine.

2. Buy a detergent made by a company that's likely to use you in a commercial.

3. Get enough cars so you can leave in one and come back in another.

4. Buddy up to the butcher if you're feeding six kids.

5. Hold off on getting an answering machine until you've ditched the rotary dial.

6. Don't invest in collars if you never see your dog.

7. Consider a deep conditioner before the back-combing, if you're a maid.

8. Collect hair bows like they were condiment packs from Taco Bell.

9. Get the perm from a professional, if you're a dad.

Dear Carol and Mike,
  So am I like your dog or what?
  Tiger

Dear Carol and Mike,
  I have written several times now and
can't get anyone in this family to
respond to me. Am I like your dog or
what?
  Tiger

## Things You'll Never See Carol Do

1. **Floors.**

2. **Yard work.**

3. **Windows.**

4. **Laundry.**

5. **Dishes.**

6. **"The Wild Thing" with Mike.**

Dear Carol,

I have never seen a haircut quite like yours. My oh my, it's as if it's blow-dried forward in one part and flipped up backward in another spot. Even on the Home Shopping Network, some of their beautiful models I see while collecting more blown glass for my seven wonderful grandchildren (oldest is sixteen and already winning on local dirt track) have not been able to duplicate this look.

I know this is like asking for a recipe, please don't think bad of me—please tell me, Carol, how in the world do you get your hair like that?

Opal Shoemake

Gauley Bridge, West Virginia

P.S. I have enclosed special photos I thought you might enjoy of my VFW Ladies Auxiliary supper. We had Bud Austin as head speaker. You know, he is knowledgeable in African Violet Club circles. Those are my amaryllis there on the right which I just brought to show off my flowers.

Hello, Opal,

Didn't you know they did my hair in makeup, an hour before we shot the show?

As for your plants, I don't do much gardening as all my time is spent sitting in the family room or the kitchen waiting to answer children's questions—and our yard seems to grow with very little maintenance.

Best of luck with your grandson.

**Carol Brady**

**Well, I'd guess I was looking at my guy, Mike, here and not Alice's pot roast—though both are outtasight, as the kiddos say.**

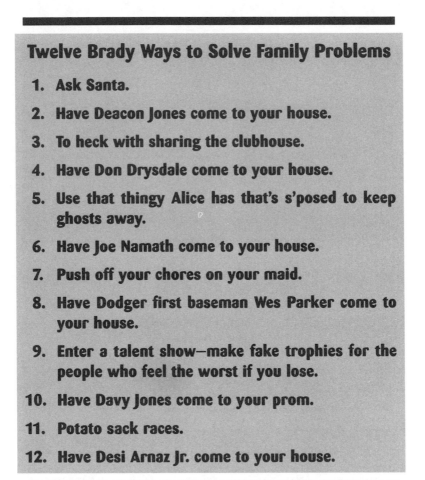

## Twelve Brady Ways to Solve Family Problems

1. Ask Santa.

2. Have Deacon Jones come to your house.

3. To heck with sharing the clubhouse.

4. Have Don Drysdale come to your house.

5. Use that thingy Alice has that's s'posed to keep ghosts away.

6. Have Joe Namath come to your house.

7. Push off your chores on your maid.

8. Have Dodger first baseman Wes Parker come to your house.

9. Enter a talent show—make fake trophies for the people who feel the worst if you lose.

10. Have Davy Jones come to your prom.

11. Potato sack races.

12. Have Desi Arnaz Jr. come to your house.

Dear Carol,

I am planning a party and am aware of your PTA work and the fact that you are attentive to your husband's needs. So maybe you can help.

Do you know the right way to mix up several shots of Sex on the Beach or a Fuzzy Navel?

Jackie

Pennsylvania

P.S. I'm right near the world's largest outlet mall, for reference.

Uh, Jackie,

First of all, there's a word we Bradys don't use in our household, and you just did.

Second, fuzz is not an issue around here due to Alice's sure use of fabric softeners and lint traps.

And finally, I don't know what this "outlet mall" deal is you talk about, but I hope they can help you clean up your language and your laundry problems.

Respectfully,

**Carol Brady**

**Watching Cindy stir up something healthy makes a mom feel pretty good. Maybe I should try it sometime.**

Dear Carol,

I've always found it remarkable that the Brady family stays so healthy! Indeed, I can't ever remember any one of your kids getting sick, except, of course, for the time they got the chicken pox or measles—whatever it was. Gosh, in my family of five, it seems at least one or two kids are always coming down with something—a cold, the flu, a broken arm,

```
you name it. It's like our house is a
hospital ward! What's your secret?
  Sincerely,
  Susan Withrow
  New Iberia, Louisiana
```

Dear Susan,

Well, we find that if our maid prepares no less than eight healthy meals a day, this seems to do the trick.

Also, an absence of toilets in our home may cut down on transferred germs. We don't seem to have many trees,

**Mike and I at the renewal of our marriage vows. Is that a handsome guy or what?**

either, which has really helped cut down on broken bones. Our kiddos are quite safe on their bikes as well and observe all rules of the roadways, as my husband Mike has taught them—oh, that guy! Though we do hold our breath with this one daughter.

**Carol Brady**

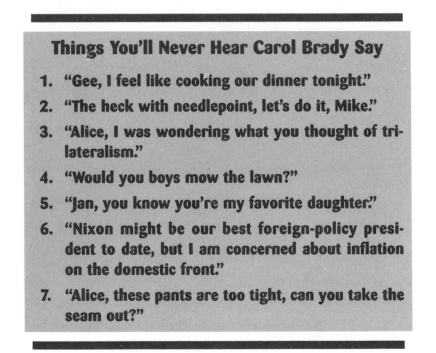

## Things You'll Never Hear Carol Brady Say

1. "Gee, I feel like cooking our dinner tonight."
2. "The heck with needlepoint, let's do it, Mike."
3. "Alice, I was wondering what you thought of trilateralism."
4. "Would you boys mow the lawn?"
5. "Jan, you know you're my favorite daughter."
6. "Nixon might be our best foreign-policy president to date, but I am concerned about inflation on the domestic front."
7. "Alice, these pants are too tight, can you take the seam out?"

Dear Carol,

I was wondering how you stay so pretty and put together, with six kids running around that house. Plus, modern worries. And you still seem to have time for needlepoint. My husband had an affair and it put a head of gray hair on me.

You are an amazing woman.

Anne

Orange County

That postman, what a guy.

Dear Anne,

You're too kind. Well, I think a happy marriage is the key to looking your best, being your best, and feeling your best. I spend so much energy on my guy Mike that, really, I don't have time to get bogged down in the worries that most women have.

Oh, sure, I'm just like everyone else—worrying when he gets home from work at 3:10 P.M. instead of 3:00 P.M. sharp. Or I have the obvious concerns when I don't feel he's getting enough reading time in bed at night.

And, of course, there's the silly little worry that I don't pay enough attention to him when he's on an important phone call.

But mostly, if I just put all my energies there, then that is energy well spent—and, as Mike always says, energy well spent is energy earned.

(Oh, that guy!)

**Carol Brady**

Dear Carol,
    I was wondering what your secret to marital success is. I married a gentleman of uncertain character but of alleged fine upbringing and it did not work out. I have two very lovely boys with hair of gold like their mother. But frankly, I'd rather give it all up to have avoided this whole mess.

His mum has always been against divorce
due to how the gawking lot will react on
the streets.
   As far as the looks go, he's a bloody
crum like your Mike.
   How do you manage to keep things going?
Dye
London


Dye,

Well, first I can see you started with good taste if your
guy looks anything like my Mike.

And I do appreciate the compliment.

I think a weekend away for you two would help fuel
those fires. Let your maid go along to take care of those
boys. After all, dear, sleeping in a different bed for a night
or two doesn't mean you can't keep working on your
hook rug or—hey, if he's got a yen for the outdoors like
my Mike, how about surprising him with an air fern in a
small pot?

Hope this helps.

**Carol Brady**

**Here we are on our last extra-special day—that, of course, would be our anniversary. What a guy.**

## Likely Bob Vila Pickup Lines to Carol Brady

1. "Avocado and harvest gold make a gorgeous laundry room combo."

2. "Say, where did you find that great wallpaper in the girls' room?"

3. "No, I don't think sixteen is too old for the boys to still be sleeping in little soldier-style, powder-blue bunk beds."

4. "I can put you a wall on the other side of that kitchen."

5. "With some quick building handiwork and the right drywall, your family will have an actual room in which to put a dinner table."

6. "Mrs. Brady, I only want to check for wallpaper peeling behind the bed."

7. "Hey, your daughter's head reminds me of my favorite leveling board."

Dear Carol,

My boyfriend Sam and I can't seem to get the hang of this sculpting stuff. I know that you are pretty nifty with this kind of thing, and I really love the fact that you have even made a few horse sculptures. So you really know how this stuff is supposed to work.

Anyway, every time Sam and I sit down to make one of those sculptures where, you know, the wet clay spins around on the thingamajig in front of you and you move your hands up and down shaping the thing, well, I start cryin', we get gunk all over ourselves, and the two of us end up back in the bedroom without getting anything sculpted.

Now that Sam is gone, I'm left all alone tryin' to figure this sculpting thing out. It's like I don't have a ghost of a chance, if you know what I mean. Please help me.

Molly
Muscle Beach, California

**This is the day my dead husband showed up unannounced. Wowee! What a start I got!**

Dear Molly,

I'll have you know that there's more to me than needlepoint and looking out for my Mike, and that's the art of sculpting. But then you already seem to know that.

For the life of me, Molly, I don't know what spinning wet clay is going to accomplish—although it sounds like something our maid, Alice, would be a whiz at. Also, I encourage you to cheer up when sculpting, because

**When Mike gets back, he'll show that Roy what's what.**

getting all sad and crying and then going to sleep is no way to finish a household project.

We Bradys are a resourceful bunch, and sometimes things can best be accomplished by putting a smile on your face before putting chisel in hand. Cheery chiseling!

**Carol Brady**

Dear Carol,
　My nickname is Twinkies and I hate it.
I think people call me that because I go
back and forth between anorexic and obese
about twice a year. Any suggestions on
how to handle that? And while I've got
you, any tips on acting?
　Ricki Pond
　Inside your living room TV


Dear Ricki,

I know exactly how you feel. My former high school boyfriend, Tank Gates, used to call me Twinkles, but I think you'd agree I came out ahead of him in the nickname game, right? I find the best way to handle anything like that is to look at it as a compliment—it means people notice you and like you.

As for the part about acting, who's acting?

**Carol Brady**

# How to Be Like **Mike**

### (Permed hair and liking your own voice are very suave-A)

**Y**ou know, some people say life is like a big tea strainer, where only the big grounds survive, but my Carol and I haven't survived on being big or even being particularly rich.

We've survived on a deeper richness—that is the richness that comes from an architectural project well done, good personal hygiene, healthy meals at regular intervals, and a little harmless planning with Beebe Gallini.

However, I digress. Just know that whatever happens, build your house or your gas station or your grocery store or your tool shed or your beauty supply store exactly alike, and their foundations will be strong. And a strong foundation is enough to withstand the toughest winds.

You know, it's enough to withstand the toughest winds even for those who say life is like a big oscillating fan and only the biggest blades get the station wagon with the wood paneling.

Love your wife, watch out for the maid, watch out for those kiddos, and watch Beebe Gallini.

However, I digress.

Mike Brady.

On to the mail.

Dear Mike,

I don't know if you have these kinds of problems, Mike, but you seem like a levelheaded guy who can feel someone else's pain and who still believes in a place called hope.

And know that I can feel your pain, too, Mike. Like the time Beebe Gallini, the cosmetics queen, came to you simply for expert help with the building of her new pink cosmetics facility—and your wife Carol, and perhaps a host of others—including Miss Gallini herself,

wrongfully suspected that there might
have been something more than a business
relationship there, Mike. I feel that
pain.

To be quite honest, Mike, I am faced
with a slate of several problems. My
lovely partner, advisor, my wife—well, I
guess you can call her our quarterback,
no, the president of our household,
Mike—we might have made what many,
including our closest neighbors here on
our avenue, believe to be a bad business
investment.

And I recall the time your little
family invested in a lovely portrait to
share through the years as a memento of
your happiness and how that investment
was destroyed when that middle dingbat
daughter of yours who doesn't know a
cosmetic pack from a fanny pack, crashed
into it on her bike, unaware that her
reluctance to wear her glasses and look
even uglier than her older sibling might
imperil her family. But I digress, Mike.
I feel your pain.

And finally, my wife and I have
weathered the storms of couplehood and I

was wondering, how do you keep the
romance alive after so many seasons?
  Mano a mano, buddy.
  Sincerely,
  Name withheld
  Washington, D.C.
  P.S. I know what it is to be scorned
about one's haircut. And that Beebe was
one hot babe, wasn't she? I'm sure the
work you did under her was not all fun.
I feel your pain.

To:    Name withheld
From:  Mike Brady
Re:    Man-to-Man Matters

Well, sir, you sound like a sincere man who is often
misunderstood. As I always say, the best investment is an
investment in your team. A man who doesn't share is as
good as teamless, and we Bradys are a team.

It sounds like you might have made an unwise investment in a family portrait. Perhaps your family has a yen
on the ol' pipes and could land a spot singing on a national telethon to raise money to recoup your investment.

Frankly, sir, as much as we Bradys value family portraits, we never discount the value of some real estate investments. I'm sure everything will turn out fine. But be careful where you put your bread (as those kiddos say), because you wouldn't want to lose your house.

As for that little matter of the little woman, I find what's best for my Carol is to always allow her time for the pursuits that give her a sense of self-worth, from needlepoint to whipping up some quick costumes for a

**Carol and I always seem to be thinking the same. Crock-Pot cookery, anyone?**

variety show.

It may be my castle, but hey, it's my gal Carol who holds the fort down—even if it is with yarn ballasts and crochet needle stakes.

Maybe your wife would enjoy going shopping sometime with our maid Alice, too.

**Hey, who says being a homemaker doesn't have its fringe benefits?**

Above all else, keep yourself at your very best by reading, perhaps a bit of *Jonathan Livingston Seagull* before bed.

Also, have you considered white shoes as an option? I know it can be a little bold, but as I tell my boys, never be afraid to be different, because being different says you're not like everyone else!

My best,

**Mike**

## Mike and Carol's Tips for Marital Success

1. Have the preacher from *Little House on the Prairie* do your wedding.
2. Bring companion animals from traditionally warring species to your ceremony.
3. Reveal nothing about your former spouse until they make the sequel.
4. Get a really girlie guy to be the clerk at your honeymoon hotel.
5. The husband should perm his hair before the fifth year of marital bliss.
6. Have a waiter pour ice down Mrs. Feldman's cleavage at your reception area.
7. Instead of going to bed, eat supper in your pajamas on your honeymoon night and grieve over the six whiny kids you left at home.
8. Talk a lot about romance, but blow it off for needlepoint once in bed.
9. The wife should change her hair color once a season.
10. Always wear lots of stuff to bed.

```
TO: Mike Brady
FROM: Ardie Harrison
   I can tell you're a man with a gift for
architecture. But what's the story on
that great-looking yard of yours? Don't
tell me those three boys of yours keep it
trimmer than the Astrodome turf. What's
your secret?
   Ardie Harrison
   Sparta, Tennessee
```

Dear Ardie,

Well, we Bradys find the best secret to any success is to act as a team and be a team, and then you can accomplish great things together.

A yard isn't just a big rug made to look like grass, just as a family isn't a big bunch of people living in a square of bricks and mortar made to look like a home.

And that's kind of the way it is with the Brady lawn. Things on the surface aren't always as they appear, sometimes they're better, sometimes worse. Sometimes they're carpet.

**Mike Brady**

**Myself and the next-door neighbor. Being neighborly is just plain friendly.**

Dear Mike,
    My dad says not to tattle. But I saw something the other day that I think I should tell. Some of the older boys have been looking in the window of our neighbors', uh, especially when Mr. Rhodes

is gone and Mrs. Rhodes is, uh, gettin'
ready for goin' to bed.

This doesn't really seem like the right
thing to do, but they keep doing it. I
know one of your kids kinda tattles
sometimes, and I was wondering if I
should tell anyone about how I've seen
them seeing Mrs. Rhodes.

J. Hinkle
Arlington, Virginia

Well, young Jay,

I'd say that while tattling is not right and can get you
into trouble, this is one instance where it just might be a
darned good idea to tell an adult. Now, since you obviously don't feel comfortable telling your folks, why don't
you just tell ol' Mike all about Mrs. Rhodes, or those boys
rather.

When you tell, that tells other people that you're a tattler. But don't you worry, son, you've done the right
thing, and I'll personally make sure Mrs. Rhodes knows
that those boys can see in her window.

Now, rest assured that I won't tattle on you, but in
order to warn Mrs. Rhodes, how about giving ol' Mike

the address, son, so I can go straighten things out.

Remember, it won't be tattling. And could you tell me what Mrs. Rhodes was wearing, so I can identify her properly when I see her?

Thanks for being a good citizen, son.

**Mike Brady**

**We Bradys believe the family that stays in a single-file line and whistles together, stays together.**

## Mike Brady's Home, Lawn, and Car Care Tips

1. Install Astroturf in your backyard. (It never needs mowing, watering, weeding, or fertilizing. Its color never fades. And it's incredibly durable: After four seasons of family potato sack races under hot studio lights, our backyard never showed any wear.)

2. Live in a California-like place where it never rains and it's always sunny and nice outside.

3. Confine all daytime family activities to the living room, kitchen, or backyard. (It not only makes camera angles easier to block and actors' marks easier to hit, it saves wear and tear on the rest of the house.)

4. Strike a deal with Chrysler so you can always drive trouble-free new cars.

5. When you do drive, just drive up or down the driveway. It saves wear on the car.

Dear Mike,
   I am a young priest in a small town. I am also a bicyclist (a pretty darned good one, I might add) and have a kinda odd burr haircut that sticks straight up.
   People think it's pretty outrageous that I run around like a banshee, and there's always lots of tongue-wagging when I am dating (it's okay, I'm Episcopal).
   You are your own man. You do your hair how you want it. You seem to work the hours you want and devote your time to whatever projects you want.
   What can I do to shut everyone up?
   Father Logan


Dear Father Logan,
   Well, we never see the minister in our area because usually everyone is looking at my lovely wife singing "Come, All Ye Faithful" on Christmas Day. So I don't exactly know what a man of the cloth should look like. But hey, if he looks like ol' Mike Brady, he can't be too bad, huh?

**Me on the set—hey, is this a Roaring Twenties-quality kind of guy or what?**

Hey, if you ever lose your voice and the big guy upstairs can't help you out, my youngest daughter has an "in" with Santa Claus.

**Mike Brady**

Dear Mike,
    I'm a forty-five-year-old father of

five who recently went through a midlife crisis. It all started late last year when I noticed my hair thinning and a bunch of wrinkles lining my face. I plain just felt old and wanted to change things. So I went out and got a tummy tuck, pectoral implants, and a face-lift. Plus, I started Rogaine treatments. I also went out and bought a fast sports car and began going to bars after work. I even started a brief, but torrid, affair with my twenty-year-old secretary.

Needless to say, none of this sat too well with my wife or neglected children. I'm happy to say I've come to my senses, sold the car, had the implants removed, and become a responsible family man again. But one thing troubles me: Can I truly be contented or will I suffer another crisis?

You seem to be the most happy, faithful, devoted, and contented family man I've ever known. What's your secret?

Sincerely,
John Moritz
Richford, Alaska

Dear John,

Thanks for the compliment. I pride myself on being a good and faithful husband, a devoted and doting father, and an all-around happy and contented family man.

What's my secret? Well, simply put, it's Brady team-work. From the moment Carol and I brought this wonderful bunch together, I've realized that to succeed, we Bradys must be a team. As a team, we can surmount any obstacle, climb any mountain, forge any ocean. When you put all the Bradys together, after all, that's quite a team! I haven't had a midlife crisis, but if I ever do, I'll turn to my teammates—to Carol, Greg, Marcia, Peter, Jan, Bobby, Cindy, and Alice (she's part of the family, too)—to help pull me through.

If you remember to enlist the support of the whole "Moritz team" when you face your next crisis, I'm sure you'll find things go much better!

Best of luck.

Your teammate,

### Mike Brady

P.S. Does that Rogaine stuff actually work? I've noticed some thinning under my perm.

**Hey, what a drag, as the kiddos say. Certain members of the Brady Bunch caught me offguard with my own Instamatic.**

```
Dear Mr. Brady,
   I continue to deal with a difficult
situation that has prompted undue
punishment from peers in opposition to
myself. While they are wrong, they are
forever reminding the public (I have an
extremely important capacity, in their
eyes) that I dumped my wife shortly
before her untimely demise, and then I
remarried. This has caused much great
pain and undue suffering for myself and
my wonderful family and the many, many,
many people I sometimes call "friend"
when necessary.
   Knute
   Somewhere inside the Beltway
```

Uh, well, Mr. Knute,

Uh, perhaps you are unaware that I, too, lost my first wife, and my boys and I still grieve. Perhaps, as we Bradys say, you should have remained a team member with the team you were on, rather than just going to the team with the nicer uniforms or the better schedule, my friend. But what's done is done, and I do feel some of your pain (funny, I've been using that expression only lately).

It sounds like despite your great influence in your job, sir, that you still have more grieving and growing up to do, and are almost as self-absorbed as my beautiful oldest daughter who I was lucky enough to inherit with my second and lovely wife, Carol.

**Mike Brady**

Dear Mr. Brady,
    You being a man who knows how to control his family, and because you take vacations with them, I was wondering how you might approach the upcoming vacation with my family.
    I have two boys and a stepdaughter from my wife's first marriage, plus my wife. I am sure, with you being well-learned, that you are aware my home city is the site of Alligatorland, Xanadu, the Gatorland Zoo, and, of course, the nearby Reptile World.
    Obviously, living here, it is very hard for my kids to be impressed by other places. As we say here in Kissimmee, once

you've done a gator, you'll do another later. (Oh, that crazy tourist bureau of ours!)

   Any ideas?

   Vince

**This was on our trip to Hawaii (not the one where Bobby was taken hostage by Vincent Price).**

Hello, Vince,

Well, you seem like the kind of man who knows what kind of man he is, and that's my kind of man. Yes, I'd say it's pretty hard to impress those kiddos of yours! We found that our kids enjoy amusement parks and trips to Hawaii. Maybe somewhere along the way you could participate in a variety show or family review.

And, hey, if you're out this way, come join us for some potato sack races or driveway basketball. We have six kids and a maid and the wife and I, but somehow I know with your five, we'll still have all the space we need.

**Mike Brady**

## Other Great Edifices Mike Brady Would Like to Take Credit for Designing

1. **Stuckey's.**
2. **IHOP.**
3. **Wienerschnitzel.**
4. **Waffle House.**
5. **Seattle Kingdome.**

Dear Mike,

I am thinking of building my own house for my family. Our budget is limited, but I want it to be special. I know you built your own house (although you are more skilled than I at this craft) and know you seemed to save some money by not including toilets in the design.

And hey, how does cramming six kids in two bedrooms and a bathroom work out for you?

Great ideas, guy!

Fletcher Counts

Syracuse

Well, Fletcher,

I always say that a family who lives together lives together and they keep living together until they aren't living together. We Bradys are a team—even when it comes to washing up in the morning, and we don't get any guff from our somewhat well-in-hand kiddos.

So, design away and best of luck. Just make sure you design a bedroom for you and the little woman (ha, ha!).

**Mike Brady**

## How to Know that You'll Never Be "Like Mike"

1. Mike never once slugged a kid, even for painting a tic-tac-toe board on bedroom wall.

2. Your wife changes clothes only once a day.

3. Things you draw or design contain variety.

4. Content with one-sentence responses.

5. You watched a sporting event instead of your wife.

6. White is for tennis shoes.

7. Drank 'til you puked.

8. Wife wears more clothes at lunch or dinner than at bedtime.

9. Kids say you suck.

10. Haggar slacks in box at folks' house.

```
Fax Page 1 of 1
To: Mike Brady
From: Ralph Leon
Mike,
   I am told you have a maid who has
remained loyal through decades of
service. Well, my maid of some thirty-
plus years appears to have begun not only
letting the water spots on the bathroom
chrome build up, but stealing from me.
   Yes, Mike, stealing from me.
   How can I thwart my help from
pilfering?
```

To: Ralph

From: Mike Brady

Well, Ralph, I'd say you have a problem. As I always say, we always have to have rules, but we always have to have justice.

Anyway, stealing has never been a problem for us because our Alice just never leaves the kitchen, except to go to the door, of course.

She's usually wiping that ol' hard-working meat loaf or fresh-squeezed orange juice off her hands, and we'd know it if she picked up anything anyway. But not our Alice.

Come to think of it, even when she's just walked in the house, Alice always seems to have sirloin or lamb chop residue on her hands.

Dear Mike,
    I was wondering: My dad says you are an architect, but we've seen your house. He wondered, did you design those Stuckey's places, too? Man, what was the deal with that roof and that geeked-out aqua?
    Poncho
    Huntsville, Alabama

Dear Poncho,

You sound like a fine young man who appreciates a good piece when he sees it. Hey, that reminds me, did I ever tell you about the time I worked for Beebe Gallini? It was strictly professional, of course.

Anyway, I digress. No, I'm sorry to say I didn't design those roadside diners, but I remain awful darned jealous of the man who did.

To be quite honest, Poncho, a man is only as good as his word and he is no more than his word. That's why, while I'd like to take credit for all the great landmarks as well, I just can't.

However, there was that little white one I told to my wife Carol about the drive-thru burger place while we were in the prematrimonial state.

**Mike Brady**

**Our neighbor with Greg and Peter. She says she likes "youngsters," whatever that means.**

Dear Mike,
  I recognize you as an astute citizen.
And an astute American father and
husband. I met both of my last two wives
on the Internet, and none of them has
worked out. Do you have any suggestions?
  Rush (Just a Harmless Little Fluffball)
  Out East


Dear Rush/Harmless,

Well, I can't question a man's choice in ladies or the choices in his life because all a man is, is who he has been, and who he has been are those he has made wives of.

As for me, I'd say to those women who married you that you always need to look your best, be your best, and you will be your best.

I am making some guesses here, but I'd darned sure guess the Internet is a beauty device my Carol would never put on her gorgeous blonde head. Especially not at bedtime when she always looks like (as the kiddos say) a real far-out chick.

Now, I know there are certain circumstances, like if your wives worked at cafeterias and other eating establishments, where an Internet was required by the laws

**We Bradys are crazy with a tilted K as you can see—here I come home and find everyone tied up by Carol's first husband.**

and ordinances of the communities of the states of this great nation. But Rush, think about it: I just bet that a grown man like you knew they wore an Internet to bed before they married you.

I'd suggest if you find any more wives interested in the Internet, that there may be more than meets the blind eye. And frankly, I bet you have a few warts, too, that they were not aware of.

As we architects say, a foundation is never seen until the house is torn down, and unless your outside is really "heavy" (as the kiddos say), then I'd suggest building your own foundation so it does not split under those shortcomings we all have.

**Mike Brady**

# The **Marcia** Files

**(Or, letters from those who would be
teen models and those who just never
found the right poncho)**

**A** good conditioner is best for every day. But on weekends, try some egg yolks, or egg yolks and mayonnaise, especially if you have a date.

Use a vinegar rinse to keep your hair extra shiny, especially before cheerleader tryouts and elections and newspaper staff announcements and casting for the school play, which you're sure to make just like me.

Sometimes, sleep with a table by your bed and your hair pressed between the table and the dictionary to give that groovy, extra-straight look just right for walking down the hall. That is, *if* you want the very best dates in the school.

And especially if you want Davy Jones to come to your prom.

**Here I am at the pool—and you can guess I always condition after chlorine.**

But don't promise anything you can't keep, either.

If you have to share a room with your sisters, see if you can't get your parents to build you a special room in the attic or in your dad's den—that is, unless your goofy brother doesn't try to do it first.

In your purse and your locker and, of course, your room, keep a mirror. And wear really tight bell-bottoms.

Jeans are for little kids like my sister Cindy. But I bet you already knew that. And remember, being a teen model is a lot of work but worth it in the long run.

Now, let's take a look at some of those letters.

```
Dear Marcia,
   I am having a party for the end of
school. My mom won't be there the whole
time, but she will be part of the time.
I'm worried because I'm afraid some of my
friends might, well, like, go all the way
in the bedrooms and my mom might come in
and find out.
   Jane Roth
   Scappoose, Oregon
```

Hey, Jane,

Well, as I see it, you could just put up some groovy love beads like my brother Greg had in his bachelor pad or something to keep your friends from going all the way into the bedrooms, and then your mom wouldn't have to worry about them messing up stuff or tracking in dirt.

Our maid Alice is the same way.

Also, I find the best way to keep the party outtasight is to have some groovy dance music. And maybe you could even plan far enough ahead to write one of your favorite musical stars to see if they could attend for free and do a number or two. I've already got Davy Jones for my school dances from here on out, but betcha could probably get a guy like Bobby Sherman or David Cassidy and they would do a *super* job. And lots of chips and Coke! Guys get hungry when they're dancing like crazy!

Don't forget to leave some *Tiger Beats* around so the gals will have some totally dreamy guys to look at when

**Here I am with my good friend Davy Jones.**

the crumbs from school don't dig dancing anymore.

Have fun and don't drink too many Mr. Pibbs!

Good luck on all your dates,

**Marcia Brady**

```
Dear Marcia,
   I'm pretty sure I'm pregnant, although
I don't know exactly for sure. When I
told my boyfriend, he started ignoring me
and won't have anything to do with me.
I'm scared. What if I am pregnant and he
never talks to me again? How will I
support me and my baby if I can't get
him back? How can I get him back, Marcia?
   Kelly Zedler
   Neshkoro, Wisconsin
```

Dear Kelly,

I find the best way to keep a guy is to keep your hair silky smooth. I usually use egg whites or mayonnaise for that teen model look. And keep those split ends trimmed—no guy can turn down a Breck girl.

**Also, brush one hundred times on each side in the afternoon—
or when you're thinking about that extra-dreamy boy with the
varsity letter.**

I also usually brush my hair one hundred times before
going to bed. And never underestimate the importance
of outtasight posture. Try walking across your mom and
dad's living room with a big book, like the dictionary,

balanced on your head. And keep an eye on the funky fashions you see the teen models wear in *Tiger Beat*. My faves are the wool ponchos.

Good luck on all your dates,

**Marcia Brady**

Dear Marcia,

My dad got in trouble a few years ago at the savings and loan where he worked. He had to go away somewhere for a long time and we didn't see him for a while.

My friends at school made fun of me then, but especially now because he doesn't work at a good job anymore and doesn't make enough money as a clerk at the plant nursery to buy me the right kind of clothes anymore.

I will be driving in a few years and Marcia—we have a *Ford Taurus* now! They are talking about a *used Acura* for me.

I have had thoughts of killing myself.
MacKenzie Lynn
Philadelphia

Dear MacKenzie,

Gee, that's a different name for a first name. First of all, I'd say don't have a cow. I mean, I know it's probably a little hard for me to relate because I get to drive that big Chrysler station wagon of my dad's wherever I want as long as it is between home and school.

All I can tell you is, there is a lot that can help when you don't have groovy clothes—like scrubbing your face twice a day and, hey, Clearasil can always make up for where the washcloth fails.

And hey, look on the bright side, if your mom can sew, maybe she can put together some groovy costumes, and you guys could do your own singing act for some extra money.

**Marcia Brady**

Dear Marcia,

I have tried throwing up. I have tried health-food products, and I have tried massive doses of diuretics and laxatives. I can't afford liposuction because I'm a freshman and too young to get a job yet.

```
But I somehow just can't get the fat off
my legs. You look so great, I hate you.
  Annette
  Long Island
```

Dear Annette,

Wow, I'm sorry to hear you've been sick, that's a real bummer throwing up.

But as for your legs, why not try Grape Nuts with grapefruit (grape and grape, sounds funny, huh?) in the morning, a Sego for lunch, and some Ayds candies in the evening. That's how I heard Susan Dey does it. Susan Dey also says never to use the washcloth you use on your body for your face, but that's another tip.

As for your stomach problems, I'd just tell your mom or your maid, and they can probably bring some Pepto Bismol up to your room or something and have you feelin' outtasight in a jif.

**Marcia Brady**

## Marcia's Guide to Staying Slender

1. Have a maid who cooks a lot, but don't ever be seen eating her food.

2. Breakfast-table-only house leaves no chance for lunch or dinner.

3. Sego.

4. Lots of walking to class.

5. Tab and Fresca.

6. Potato sack races.

7. Flicking hair often.

8. Sigh at middle sister until anaerobic.

**I couldn't do anything with my hair this day, but for some reason Greg thought I looked super. Can you imagine?**

Dear Marcia,
   I was at my school dance a few weeks
ago and I left to go to the parking lot
with these three boys. One thing led to
another, and I think I went too far with
them. Now I feel awful.
   Betty Ann Stout
   Burleson, Texas


Dear Betty Ann,
   I always say it's best never to go steady with more than
two boys at once.
   Good luck on all your dates,
   **Marcia Brady**

Hi, Marcia,
   Hey, I got this problem. My mom won't
let me watch *Beavis and Butt-head*. She
says they are a bad influence. What would
you do?
   Rachael Marie Conti
   Cambridge, Massachusetts

Well, Rachael, I don't know these guys from school. Maybe they are seniors or something. But all I know is, I would never, ever date a guy named Beavis —and I sure wouldn't date a guy with, uh, that other name. Maybe you should stick to guys in your class. There's some

**Here I am on just about the grooviest day ever. Can you imagine, me, Last Day of School Queen?**

juniors with names like Warren or Doug I really dig.

Good luck on all your dates,

**Marcia Brady**

## Eight Reasons Marcia Brady Would Not Make It Today as a Teen Model

1. **Throwing up is for when you're sick.**

2. **Backcombing is for moms.**

3. **Davy Jones no longer has connections.**

4. **Doesn't wear jeans.**

5. **Promotional schedule conflicts with talent show.**

6. **No potato sack races in Paris.**

7. **Socializing difficult—super models prefer wine and celery to malteds and Alice's pot roast.**

8. **Cheryl Tiegs has Sears gig wrapped up.**

```
Dear Marcia,
  Am I like your dog or what?
  Tiger
```

**Hey, here I am again brushing my hair—one hundred times a night, as usual—and with a really neato brush, as usual.**

Hi, Marcia,
   I'll be, like, seventeen next month, and for sure I've had my driver's license now, like, for-ever. My dad says he trusts me, but, Marcia, he won't let me drive his Range Rover to school until I'm eighteen. Marcia, what should I do?
   LeighAnn Miller
   Long Beach

Hi, LeighAnn,

Well, I'm not sure what a Range Rover is. I've never heard my brother Greg talk about them and he knows all about cars, even though I beat him in a driving test because I didn't break an egg my dad set on this cone thing. But a Range Rover, isn't that some kind of Jeep or something?

That's kinda creepy, LeighAnn, our mailman drives a Jeep. Maybe you should save up for something way out like a Mustang II or a LeSabre (great for taking your best friends to the pizza parlor). Or it might seem like a real drag, but Warren Mulaney drove his mom's Gremlin for a while and it never broke down or anything, except it always ran out of gas at Frenchman's Point.

With a few far-out flower stickers, any creepy car can be a dream machine.

Bet the guys will go bananas.

Good luck on all your dates,

**Marcia Brady**

**This is me and my friend. For some reason, she doesn't really think the boys I like are really a good thing.**

Hello, Marcia,

My name is Corina Soto. I am from Bakersfield, California. In a few months I will be having something called a *quinceanera*. In the Hispanic community, it is a very important day for young women because it is sort of like the day we go from being little girls to grownups. We have something called a *merienda,* which is a tea, and then a *jarape* (dance), and finally we have a mass at church and a party. I am really excited, but my mom says we can't afford anything more than a deejay or a neighborhood band because the dresses and food are so much. And if I do have a real band, she says, because of how important this is, they can't be anything but a Latin band that reflects well on our heritage.

Corina

Dear Corina,

Gee, I'm not sure. That's a pretty big problem. I don't know much about this holiday you're talking about. And we don't go to church except when my mom loses her voice on Christmas Eve.

My brother Greg sings as Johnny Bravo—is Bravo like a Spanish name?

Hey, once Desi Arnaz Jr. came to my house after I wrote in my diary that I loved him. I think his dad had a band that might have reflected some kind of heritage, but

**Here I am teaching my brother Greg how to dance. He seems to like having a sister he can dance with.**

I'm not sure what.

Good luck on all your dates,

**Marcia Brady**

P.S. Does this party mean you're old enough to go steady?

Dear Marcia,
Can I please be your dog only? Your gym shirts smell the best of anyone, ever.
Tiger

Dear Marcia,
I live in an apartment house with just two bedrooms. Except for my two little baby sisters, the rest of us (five and Holler, that's my uncle's dog) sleep on one mattress in one bedroom. Everybody's always fighting and coming in at all hours. I am thinking of running away. What should I do, Marcia?
Pam Diethorn
Pittsburgh

Dear Pam,

Oh, I know what you mean. I've been dealing with this for a while, and I know it is really tough to get your beauty sleep when you have to share a bedroom. My sisters and I have three twin beds in our room, and I, being the oldest, of course, and having to look my outtasight best all the time, have had to make sure the younger girls stick to the schedule I've figured out.

If you want to keep looking your teen model best, then I suggest doing what we do and taking turns, where the oldest gets the mirror first and I brush my hair one hundred times—sometimes on each side. Then we take turns where the oldest gets the bathroom first and I wash my hair in Breck shampoo three times and condition twice with eggs and mayonnaise.

Then you should take turns where the oldest gets the desk first and I do my homework, usually about a half-hour, which is all I need to make an A, plus extra credit.

Then the youngest goes, and last, of course, the one in the middle.

Good luck on all your dates,

**Marcia Brady**

# **Grego** y Grego

### (Or, how vinyl jackets make
### great ego stuffers)

If you wanna go out with outtasight chicks, there is only one way to be groovy—be like me, Greg Brady.

I taught myself everything I know. You gotta have the moves down, the hair down, and the shirt and pants down.

But, hey, I go groovin' way off here. Just give me a sailboat and a moonlit night, and chicks will supply themselves.

On parents, you just gotta be smooth enough to make 'em think you're listening, and just groovin' enough to be your own guy and never take your little brother on a date.

Here's some advice I live by and know you oughta, too—Greg Brady is a man who blow dries his own hair. Next up, some pretty cool letters addressed to one cool dude.

```
Dear Greg,
   Like, I know you're really, like, into
music, and I was wondering, like, what
bands do you like? You know, like, my
favorite band is the Stone Temple Pilots
'cause they're totally rad and I really
like their music. Plus, I really like
Smashing Pumpkins.
   Jammin' in the Valley,
   Jimi Cleek
   San Bernardino, California
```

Dear Jimi,

I really dig the Stones, too. Mick Jagger always has the hippest threads and tightest jeans. I wish I could sing like him, too, 'cause the girls really dig him. As far as smashing pumpkins goes, that kind of thing just doesn't happen in the Brady neighborhood. Come to think of it, we've never celebrated Halloween in our neighborhood.

Keep on truckin',

**Greg Brady**

Dear Greg,
  My girlfriend is really tired of my old Nissan 280ZX and wants me to get a new car. Got any suggestions?
  Sincerely,
  Barton Withrow
  Houston, Texas

**Hey, hot bell-bottoms and a cool car equals chicks, as you can see.**

Dear Barton,

I'm not sure what kind of car you're driving, but I'll tell you, man, nothin' beats an American car!

The new Ford Mustang is really hot and so is the new Pontiac GTO. And you can't go wrong with the groovy-looking new Camaro. Of course, if you go to the beach, nothing beats a VW bus for hauling surf boards, picnic baskets, and a bunch of friends. (Plus, it doubles as a great bachelor pad on wheels!) Of course, we Bradys really like Chryslers. They're all Dad ever drives, and they're the only thing you'll see me drive!

Happy car hunting,

**Greg Brady**

Dear Greg,

What's with your hair? It was straight and short at first when you were younger (kinda like Robbie's on *My Three Sons*). But as you've grown it has just gotten longer, curlier, and more goofy looking. Your sideburns are okay, but you oughta cut your hair like Jason on *90210*. My

husband keeps his hair real short and it
looks great that way.
    Jenny Gump
    Greenbow, in the county of Greenbow,
    Alabama


Dear Jenny,

Thanks for your letter. Short hair might be the style in Greenbow and on whatever street your friend Jason lives. But where I come from, long curly hair is the *in thing*! And the girls totally dig me for it! Your husband ought to hang loose a bit and grow his hair out!

My dad's an older guy and kinda square, but he let his hair grow out. He even got it permed to get that mod Afro look.

Sincerely,

**Greg Brady**

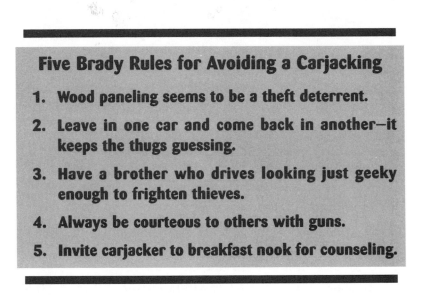

**Five Brady Rules for Avoiding a Carjacking**

1. **Wood paneling seems to be a theft deterrent.**

2. **Leave in one car and come back in another—it keeps the thugs guessing.**

3. **Have a brother who drives looking just geeky enough to frighten thieves.**

4. **Always be courteous to others with guns.**

5. **Invite carjacker to breakfast nook for counseling.**

Dear Greg,
  So, am I like your dog or what?
  Tiger

Dear Greg,
  I've been, like, doin' this girl behind my girlfriend's back and now she says she is pregnant and wants me to marry her. I

don't think she's really got a bun in the
oven, but, hey, man, if she spills it to
my girlfriend, I'm, like, a dead man. I'm
just clueless about what to do, man. Can
you cop me some plan?
  Derik M.
  San Bernardino, California


Dear Derik,

Man, I really dig the way you talk. *Very cool, very heavy.* But, hey, if I understood you right, you said you might have gotten a girl pregnant. That's *way uncool.* You need to tell your parents right away and get their advice. As my father once told me: "Greg, everything you do reflects on you, and if what you do doesn't reflect good on you then that's a bad reflection on you." I think you need to look at how a pregnant girl reflects on you and do the right thing.

  Best of luck,

  **Greg Brady**

**This is my surfer pose for the chicks at the beach. They were really blown away—especially when they heard my dad was gonna maybe let me make his study into a bachelor pad.**

Dear Greg,
  I know you're kind of a budding
guitarist. So am I. I've been looking
forward to getting a new guitar, but I
can't decide on whether to get an
acoustic or electric guitar. I'm kind of
leaning toward a Fender Stratocaster. The
local music store has them on special.
Any suggestions?
  Sincerely,
  John Carlson
  Amherst, Massachusetts


Dear John,

  I think an electric guitar is the grooviest way to go. I
tried an acoustic guitar once and hated it. It made me
look like Art Garfunkel with dark hair. I'm not familiar
with the Fender Stratocaster, but if the price is right and
you like it, you ought to get it.

  Keep on groovin' to the music.

  **Greg Brady**

### Greg's Top Pickup Lines

1. "Wanna be my potato sack race partner?"
2. "Who's your favorite Monkee? Did I mention Davy Jones came to my house once and we rapped?"
3. "That's a really mod dress you're wearing. Is it Quiana?"
4. "Well, yes, but Jan Brady isn't my blood relative."
5. "Hey, I have my own pad in my parents' attic."
6. "Hey, wanna hear my new Banana Generation eight-track? We can listen to it in my station wagon."
7. "Yes, that's right. I am David Cassidy."
8. "Did you know Marcia Brady is my sister? We're really close. I can tell you how she gets her hair like that."
9. "No, really, Jan and I have different moms."
10. "Did anyone ever tell you, you look just like Peggy Lipton?"
11. "I was once asked to sing backup for the Cowsills."
12. "Hey there, groovy chick."

**Hey, does Davy Jones have anything to compare with this or what?**

Dear Greg,
(c/o the Brady Bunch Fan Club)
   I've always admired your taste in clothes. Those body-hugging knit shirts really show off your rock-hard abs and pecs. And you look so-o-o-o-o good in tight jeans. I'm kind of a husky, big bear of a guy, but really nice and gentle. I'd like to get lean and sexy like you. Can you tell me how you keep so fit and where you get your clothes? Do you pick them out yourself?
   Your biggest fan,
   Paul P.
   San Francisco
   P.S. Can I have your address so I can write you a more personal letter?


Dear Paul,

   Thanks for the compliments. You sound like a groovy guy with great taste. I pick out all my clothes myself from Sears and Chess King, but I'm sure you can find mod threads like mine at any "with it" men's store in your town.

I stay fit with daily potato sack races and chasin' chicks. As you've probably noticed, we Bradys eat very little, and that helps us all stay trim.

Sorry, I can't give out my home address. You sound like a really nice guy, but it's against my dad's policy.

Thanks for writing,

**Greg Brady**

P.S. Do you have a beard? I'm thinking of growing one.

```
Dearest Greg,
(c/o The Brady Bunch Fan Club)
  I do have a beard—a big fuzzy, sexy one
I know you'd like!
  But please, don't you grow a beard!
You've got a wonderful, fresh-scrubbed,
boyish-hunk-type face. You should never
cover it up! In fact, I've often thought
of shaving my beard off (leaving long
sideburns) to be more like you!
  Your biggest fan,
  Paul P.
  San Francisco
  P.S. Thanks for the fitness advice!
```

Those daily potato sack races are tough!
I've already dropped ten pounds and am
feeling great. I'm having problems
finding clothes like yours, though. But
that's okay, I've got a few more pounds
to lose before I could wear them anyway.

Dear Greg,
  I'm just totally in love with your
sister Marcia. I'd love to meet her and
maybe go out on a date.
  Terin Miller,
  Lovesick in Belle Fourche, South Dakota

Dear Terin:
  I know how you feel.
  Good luck,

**Greg Brady**

  P.S. She might go out with you if you're a high school
quarterback or if you deliver wallpaper to our house.

**Here's Marcia and me. I don't remember much about this picture because I had to leave when something suddenly came up.**

Dear Greg,
   There isn't a lot to do around here,
but I know you probably know the best
place to take a chick and what to wear
and how to act to be really cool. Most
of the girls here won't, like, well, you
know, until at least the second date.
   And even then, her folks or my folks
need to be gone, or in the summer there's
the grain elevator.
   Dave Rieckmann
   Indiana


Hey, Dave,

Far-out for asking the right guy. If you want a girl to
think you're really heavy, start with the look. Always
wear tight pants and a white belt and white shoes no
matter what season it is—or if you're in a climate-
controlled studio.

I'd try the pizza parlor first. Then the ice cream shop—
a double dip if you're really wanting things to get heavy.
A little Hai Karate helps, too. Be careful where you
splash 'cause this flashy knit stuff your jackets better be

made out of doesn't wash easy, or so says our maid (who works for free).

Tell this chick you think she's a cinch for cheerleader and, man, you are on your way to settin' that arm around the shoulder, pal.

A little moonlight and a yacht or a bachelor pad and you're on your way.

**Greg Brady**

**Hey, it must not be the pants, huh? This is me with chicks all over me because of my singing voice.**

Say, Grego,

I have been seeing your clothes for a while and was wonderin', do you have to, like, wear Garanimals or something to get your clothes that tight?

Lance
Stuck with Dad, stationed in Italy

Hey, Lance,

Cool to hear you dig my threads. Man, I don't know what these Garanimals are, but they sound outtasight. Hey, that's not like those Paul Revere and the Raiders threads, is it?

**Greg Brady**

Dear Greg,

Just had to write you back. Dude, have a clue. I don't mean I like your clothes just because I look at them. Man, take a look around, buddy—at some point didn't you, like, get a hint that maybe it's not

```
cool for your dress shirts to fit like a
latex contraceptive device—dig it, '70s
boy.
   Lance
```

```
Dear Greg,
   Everybody thinks Marcia is really hot
stuff, but I think Jan is the number-one
babe in your house. I thought Jan looked
especially hot in the red zipper top and
plaid bell-bottoms she wore that time
Marcia broke her nose. How can I meet
Jan?
   Jan's biggest fan,
   Bruce Mottl
   Fort Dodge, Iowa
```

Hey, Bruce,

You're not sniffin' glue, are you? I mean, Jan a hot chick? C'mon, our dog doesn't even like her. My dad says she's gotta grow up some to groove to her self-confidence. Still, I wonder how that'll help the dog thing. Say, have you ever seen my older sister Marcia? Actually, you and Jan might hit it off pretty well, because it sounds like you both won't wear your glasses.

Thanks for writing,

### Greg Brady

P.S. If you're really serious about Jan, you should write her directly. I'm sure she'd love to meet someone who likes her better than Marcia.

Dear Greg,
   So, man, how was it you were able to avoid the draft? Weren't you, like, in high school while we were still in Nam?
   I'm sitting here with a good job, but no legs and no thanks to pretty boys like you.
   So what did you do in the '70s, spend a decade trying to get your shirt peeled off?
   Lieutenant Dan
   Lake Havasu City

**Hey, do you think this guy looks like me?**

Dear Dan,

Hey, man, I'm not sure what the heck you're talking about, but it sounds pretty heavy. Maybe this is one you better be asking your parents about.

**Greg Brady**

Dear Greg,

I am a sophomore at the University of Wisconsin (picture enclosed). Some people say I'm kinda cute. But it's a little hard to be cute here in Antarctica when you're, like, wearing a comforter, a mattress, and four pairs of socks to class. Dear God, I look like Snoopy in the Macy's parade. Do you have any ideas for good schools to relocate to in a warmer climate?

Susan
Madison, Wisconsin

**Here I am on the way to Hawaii. Stewardesses really dig it when I play chords.**

Hey, Susan,

Wow, I dig that happenin' name. Like your long golden hair in that picture. Relocate with Greg Baby, and you'll always be burnin' hot, and I can teach you plenty.

**G. B.**

**Marcia and I have always been very close. Don't we look groovy here?**

**My brother Peter and I enjoy airplane flights almost as much as we do Judge Roy Scream at Six Flags!**

# On Being **Jan**

**(Or, how three feet of blonde hair
and a skeletal system are terrible
things to waste)**

If anyone tells you that you aren't as good as your sister or anyone else, just don't listen to them because you are probably outtasight on your own.

And if you have to wear glasses like I do, it doesn't mean you're a bad person, even if you are ugly like me.

And if your Keds fit you funny like mine do, it doesn't mean you won't get elected to any offices at school or will fail to get into any clubs like me.

Also, if your older sister has better hair and gets dreamier guys, it doesn't mean you're a loser. Then again, I never get dates and my shoes fit funny and I have never won anything except an essay contest, which I had to give up because they figured the score wrong and Nora Coombs really won.

**No one ever believes anything was my idea at first. Here is where I think I was telling my brothers and sisters how I invented foam curlers.**

Hmm, really I guess that means I'm a loser. I guess you are, too, if that happens to you.

I really don't know what to do unless I get my hair colored different or a wig or get more mod with my bod, as my brother Greg might say.

I don't know how I'll ever be like Marcia. Oh, dear God, doesn't anyone out there understand me? Please, write me and tell me if you do.

Stop me. Somebody stop me.

I swear, I swear I'll run off. I swear I'll run off with one of Peter's friends if nobody will listen to me.

No, I know, I'll run off with Joe Namath. He came to

visit Cindy and Bobby. I know he'll visit me. That's it, I'll run off with Joe Namath. He'll throw a football that will hit Marcia in her fat face and it will be right before prom night and . . .

Oops, excuse me, I was dreaming. Of course, I was just dreaming about how nice and tasty Alice's tuna noodle casserole will be this evening. Now, let's see what's in my mail slot.

Dear Jan,

My mom says we don't have role models today. I was wondering what you think of this. She says I have poor role models. Mostly they are sports stars, especially this one basketball player you might not know because you are a girl, and a middle child at that, but she doesn't like him because he always dyes his hair a different color and does some other strange stuff.

I am thinking of dying my hair, like, pink or something. I seem to remember you dyed your hair a different color one time, and I was wondering if it was bad

influences that made you do that and if
you would do it again.
  Jeff K.
  Chicago

Oh, dear Jeff,

  Oh, my, yes, it was terrible influences that caused my
hair color to change, terrible influences. No one under-

**This is my counselor. Even she doesn't understand about
wearing glasses.**

stands me. I can see, they just make me wear glasses to make me uglier than Marcia—always Marcia, Jeff.

Jeff, Jeff, Jeff, always Marcia. I'll show them, I'll join the Partridge Family. The bus would understand me.

Yes, I changed my hair color. Yes, I wore a black wig, and they all made fun of it. All of them made fun of me.

It was a terrible scene that made me wear a brunette wig, Jeff. No one understands me, not even my biological father, Reuben Kinkaid. Yes, I'm sure that's who it was.

Oh, anyway, what was it you were asking, Jeff?

Hope this helps, and do you have a sister in the Sunflower Girls? My brother Peter had to wear my Sunflower outfit once. Maybe that would help your identity.

### Jan Brady

P.S. Do you think if I ran away, Sonny Bono would marry me?

Dear Jan,
   All my friends have their navels and nipples pierced. My mom says I can get my ears pierced one more time (that's four) but nothing else. How am I supposed to

get noticed by any guys now—get a tattoo
of a friggin' joint across my forehead or
what? It's like no one even sees me going
down the hall.
  Nina Cherry
  Clearwater, Florida


Dear Nina,

I can't imagine why you'd want to do any of those
things you talk about. Yucca-doo. A short black wig
would probably be the best thing to set you apart from all
your blonde sisters and help you make pompon girl and
do something better than your horribly perfect sister.

**Jan Brady**

Dear Jan,
  Just had to write you back. I never
said I had a sister, and my hair is
magenta.
  Nina

Dear Jan,

My sisters and I own a bakery together. Our macaroons are the best, but Jan, I am the middle of three grown daughters and frankly, I think this hampers my ability to decorate cakes, clean the utensils, and get men. They say I can't park good, either. Can you help me?

Pamela Sue Austin

Lawrence, Kansas

P.S. Hey, is it true what I heard that

**Here I am showing Marcia my annual. I bet she doesn't realize that "How do you ever keep your ear hair kinked up like that?" is a compliment.**

Marcia knows seven languages, including
Catalonian and Portuguese, and once had
her picture made with Dawn from Tony
Orlando, and a talent scout thought she
was a bunch prettier than Dawn?

Dear Pam,

I know you can understand what it is like to be here in
the middle. I say you have to set yourself apart. I bet your
sisters are blonde. I bet their hair does better than yours. I
bet you hate them and wish they'd never been born.

I think you should run away and get on a semi truck
with someone who looks like your childhood maid.

Everyone else will abandon you. Your real dad. Even
your dog, Pam.

No one even cares if I ever learn how to drive. Especially not Marcia. Oh, God, no, I said that name.

Marcia. Marcia. Marcia. Darn her hair. Darn her hair.

I'm running away tonight, that's it.

Hope this helps a lot.

## Jan Brady

P.S. If I ran away do you think the blond guy on *Here
Come the Brides* would marry me?

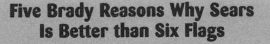

## Five Brady Reasons Why Sears Is Better than Six Flags

1. **Family musical numbers more easily choreographed on escalators.**

2. **Bell-bottoms.**

3. **Cindy and Bobby tall enough to ride elevators.**

4. **Roller coaster hell on long hair.**

5. **Amusement park setup makes for more expensive set.**

Dear Jan,
   You're a nice sister for Cindy and Marcia and all, but I know you're busy and don't have a lot of time, so you don't need to ever pet me or come near me with that bike, especially not near my house.
   Tiger

P.S. Would you ask Marcia to make me another one of those cool decoupage doghouse plaques? She is real talented.

Dear Tiger,

Why, yes, Tiger, I want you to be my dog and my dog only. I think you're the only one who understands me around here.

**Jan Brady**

Dear Jan,

Hey, in the start of the show where it shows your faces, do you have, like, a *thing* on your forehead or something?

Ethan M.

DeSoto, Missouri

P.S. Hey, did Marcia put, like, a special conditioner on her hair to make it that shiny in that shot?

**Here I am at the pool. As you can probably guess, Marcia is near me. What does Marcia have that I don't? Except a bunch of spelling trophies—and Last Day of School Queen trophies and Best of Show trophies and stuff.**

Dear Ethan,

Why is everyone always picking on me? What did I ever do but be born? No one even thinks I can do anything, not even homework. Marcia doesn't even have to do her homework. She just has it in her head. Cindy doesn't *have* homework.

I'm last in the bathroom, every morning. Do you think three boys need to be before me in the bathroom?

I'm going to run away. That's it.

**Jan Brady**

P.S. If I ran away, do you think that blond guy from *The Man from U.N.C.L.E.* would marry me?

Dear Jan,

My mom does volunteer work for Lighthouse for the Blind and wondered if you would write back and tell us if you would help us with a fund-raiser.

Carol Solberg

Gila Bend, Arizona

P.S. Hey, would you ask your sister Marcia what she uses on her hair? I want

to get mine just like that by the time
I'm twelve.

**I know now that I really *can* be a teen model more than Marcia.**

Dear Carol,

Why, of course, I'd love to help. I'd love to be a teen model for your talent search fund-raiser. That would be totally outtasight.

Just write me any time—write me several times.

**Jan Brady**

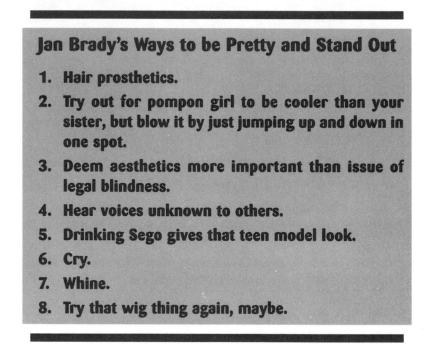

## Jan Brady's Ways to be Pretty and Stand Out

1. **Hair prosthetics.**
2. **Try out for pompon girl to be cooler than your sister, but blow it by just jumping up and down in one spot.**
3. **Deem aesthetics more important than issue of legal blindness.**
4. **Hear voices unknown to others.**
5. **Drinking Sego gives that teen model look.**
6. **Cry.**
7. **Whine.**
8. **Try that wig thing again, maybe.**

**You can see me here, so obviously I don't need glasses.**

Dear Jan,

We got your letter back about our Lighthouse for the Blind thing. Uh, your talent wasn't exactly what we had in mind, my mom says.

Thanks for your offer anyhow, and we'll find another spokesperson, my mom says. She also said to tell you that you are viewing your impairment through rose-colored contacts.

Carol
Gila Bend, Arizona

Dear Jan,

When I was younger, I tried holding my breath until I died to get attention, but I couldn't do it long enough. Now I'm thinking of just hitting myself on the arm with something and bruising it and saying my brothers did it because they'll never believe I'd do something like that and will believe me instead of my brothers—and then they'll have to doctor me.

My friends think this is sick, but if
it works, who cares?
What do you think?
Brittany Gonzalez
Asheville, North Carolina

**Here's me and a friend. I bet Marcia doesn't have a special
friend like this.**

**This is my friend George Glass. He doesn't need glasses either—**
*and he is a real guy.*

Hi, Brittany,

Gee, what an unusual name, Brittany. Oh no, I wouldn't hold your breath until you died. It's not worth it just to get someone to pay attention to you.

Say, you say you are having trouble getting anyone to pay attention to you? Gee, a bruised arm would really make someone stand out and get attention. I wonder how much more attention I—I mean you—could get by breaking your arm all the way.

That's it. That'll show 'em all. I'll break my arm and I'll do it right before Marcia's class elections. But she'd just probably win anyway because everyone would feel sorry her sister's arm was broken and vote for her. I'll show 'em; I'll break my leg. Yes, that's it!

Hope this helps.

**Jan Brady**

# Peter's
# Middle View

**(Or, how scant character development
can help you survive those
challenging, voice-changing,
middle-school years)**

**M**y brother Greg says he is a guy who blow dries his own hair. Heck, you wanna know the truth? Some days he doesn't even blow dry his hair. And he looks really creepy when he gets out of bed, too.

That's what you gotta remember, even if your brother or somebody else seems like a groovy guy, it doesn't mean you aren't a groovy guy, too.

And if you're thirty or somethin' and still having to share a bunk bed with your little brother, that's okay, too.

My dad says what is inside you is what matters, and my dad's usually right-on about that stuff. And if your mom still buys your clothes, it doesn't matter as long as you still have cool clothes.

And if you've got a bunch of crummy girls for sisters, that's okay, too. But it's only okay if you make good grades and play sports, and no one says you sing like a girl or anything. Let me share with you now some of my mail.

Dear Peter,
   Did anyone ever tell you that your clothes make you look like a total goober? No one wears that kind of stuff anymore. You look like you're from *Benny Hill* or something. Did it ever occur to you that Levis aren't supposed to fit like the childproof seal on the Tylenol bottle?
   Man, I'm from a small town, but even here we've got enough sense to turn on, like, MTV or somethin' and see what other people born after the invention of, like, cable or somethin' look like.
   Just something for you to try to think about, if brain matter equals earwax and you can.

Geez, dude, where do you even find
those clothes?
Joey Funke
North Platte, Nebraska

Dear Joey,

I don't happen to like what you're sayin'. My mom picks my clothes out and it just so happens that she has very good taste. My dad is kinda goofy sometimes, but like he said, you can tell because she married him.

**Peter Brady**

Dear Peter,
Got your letter back from my letter.
And just had to write back. Geez, your
mom picks your clothes out? Are you,
like, gay or something? And your mom—what
is the deal with her friggin' hair
anyway?
Joey Funke
The guy in Nebraska

Dear Joey,

My dad says that being different means you're not afraid to be like everyone else. And my brother Greg dresses just like me and he had a date with a cheerleader. She even did cheers in our living room.

You probably dress like some kind of hippie or somethin'.

Your drippy letter was so funny I forgot to laugh.

**Peter Brady**

Dear Peter,

    Some of my friends have a crush on Susan Dey, but I'm scared to tell 'em the truth. See, I'm not exactly interested in girls.

    Your friend (maybe more than?),
    Douglas H.
    Cleveland

**I look crummy here, maybe because I'm in school.**

Hi, Doug,

Well, sure I'll be more than a friend. My dad says you can never have too many friends, because what a man is, is what he does, and what a man does is only what he does for others, and they are his friends.

And, yeah, I gotta tell ya, I know just what you mean, I don't exactly like girls, either, and I have a secret, too: My friends all think Susan Dey is a really mod girl. But I don't go in for girls—I think Shirley Jones is a really all-together chick. I know she's older, but she's just really neat and has four kids and has a really groovy shape even in those Partridge Family threads and she can dance real good.

I think it's great we think alike. Maybe you can come hang out with me if you're ever in town since we probably could have some really far-out fun.

**Peter Brady**

Dear Peter,

Got your letter and just had to write you back soon. I'm a little scared about trying this but know I want to. I think

I could save enough money from where I work as a children's show choreographer at the local amusement park to come meet you in a month.
　Doug
　Cleveland

Dear Doug,
　Hey, that would be outtasight. And don't be scared. I, too, was scared the first time I took an airplane anywhere.
　See ya, buddy.

**Peter Brady**

**Gee whiz, I wish guys would quit takin' my picture when I'm doin' somethin' goofy. Who says it was a girl?**

Dear Peter,
　So am I like your dog or what?
　Tiger

## Peter's Tips for Surviving as a Middle Child

1. Never agree to take your sister to a birthday party.

2. If you can help it, don't join the school choir until after your voice changes.

3. If you can arrange it, have a dorky middle sister who makes you look like a totally cool middle child.

4. Have a goofy younger brother who gets stuck with all the stupidest plot lines and dialogue, so you'll look and sound cool.

5. Have a goofy older brother who thinks he's cool but is just a big dork who wishes he was David Cassidy. That will make you look cool, too.

6. Get on a hit TV show and become a teen magazine heartthrob. That way, even if no one in your family pays attention to you, thousands of girls from around the country will write you fan letters.

**Greg and Marcia made me put this in—Okay, so I got kissed!**

Dear Peter,
  My big brother had to go away to stay at a place for a while because he was so bad in school and did some other stuff. They say it's called Creekwood or Forest Groves or something like that.
  I'm not sure I really understand it,

and I don't know if he'll ever come back
or what.
   Jillian
   Auburn, Maine


Hi, Jillian,

Well, I'm not sure I know, either, but I think this could be pretty serious because once when my family went to Hawaii for vacation, my brother Bobby wandered off through this coconut grove and got kidnapped in a cave by the guy who played Dr. Phibes.

**Peter Brady**

Dear Peter,
   I'm a real good baseball player except
I'm kinda scared of the ball. Man, dude,
I don't know what I'd do if anybody else
on the team found out. I saved a no-
hitter once with a diving catch, but I'm
still scared. What should I do?
   My parents even almost named me after
this guy named Rogers Hornsby.
   Mike G.
   Colorado Springs

**Here's me and Bobby looking at dolls in Hawaii. Greg thinks his little brothers are goofy, but I think he's only half right.**

Dear Mike,

Well, what always worked best for me was to have Don Drysdale come to my house.

**Peter Brady**

**Here's where I remember thinking two things: 1) I hope this hardhat is solid, and 2) Where can a guy go to the bathroom around here?**

Dear Peter,
  Who do you think is hotter, Jennifer
Aniston or Courteney Cox?
  Randy Tinney
  Toronto


Dear Randy,

Well, I'm not sure who you mean. Are they seventh-graders or somethin'? I kinda like Julie Newmar and Peggy Lipton, who are way outtasight.

**Peter Brady**

# Cindy's
# View from Below

### (Or, if you smile real big and lisp
### until you spit, your hair will knot up
### like a razorback's tail)

**W**ell, once my Kitty Karry-All got looth and I didn't think I could go on. And once my mom and my new dad went on their honeymoon and I cried becausth we got yelled at, at the wedding justh because our cat Fluffy got loosth after the boys' mean ol' dog chased it. It was a dumb dog anyway and she didn't yell at the boys like she yelled at usth.

What worked best was to whine until they left on their honeymoon and got us. Winning a jacks conteth is different. You shouldn't cry because if you do good you win.

A brother can be okay if he's your age and you don't

have anybody your age to play with. If he ever gets thad, have a famouth football player come to your house—it's easy as jacksth! And never, ever tell when you see thome-one else hath done thomething wrong. That makes you a tattler. Don't tell, unleth a grownup makes you or it's thomething just too good not to tell.

Here are thome of my favorite letters.

```
Dear Cindy,
    I don't want to use my name, but I will
say that I was a really popular guy, a
great athlete, and I won big awards in
school. Lately, some of my friends have
been accusing me of some pretty serious
things. I'm a little older than you, but
I'm kinda upset because I remember you
were a tattletale. Well Cindy, I swear I
didn't do what they say I did—and they
are still saying it. Cindy, what makes
people tattle? What makes you tattle? I
just don't understand. Why are people
still tattling on me?
    Cindy, I just do not understand the
```

```
motivation. If it would make any
difference, I would get down on my knees
and beg you or anyone not to tattle.
Well, if I could get down on my knees.
  Name withheld
  L.A.
  P.S. Why didn't you ever have O.J. on
that show? Y'all had Deacon Jones and Joe
Namath and Don Drysdale and even the
Dodger first baseman Wes Parker who no
one's ever heard of and wouldn't know
what to do with a Heisman if it broke
into his house and took his wife, but no
O.J. What gives?
```

Dear Name withheld,

I think you might be thomewhat confuthed becauth we had orange juice all the time on the show. Alith would squeeth it fresh for our breakfast.

I sure learned my lethon when I tattled on our maid Alith hugging the mailman and her boyfriend Sam wouldn't take her to the dance.

**Throwing a ball is a great part of a fund-raisther for your dad's taxes.**

Thomehow I kinda think what you got tattled on for was even worse than Alith hugging the mailman or my brother Bobby using the pepper-shaker lid to sthrain his guppy water.

Maybe you better tell your parents.

**Thindy Brady**

Dear Cindy,
    Both my parents work and then have other stuff like their health club, and my mom goes to all kinds of classes. Now I hear my little brother is in counseling, his grades are dropping, he's skipping school, and his therapist says it's because he doesn't get enough attention.
    I don't have enough money to get him a season pass to Six Flags or buy him more toys like my parents do. What can I do to help?
    Stuart
    College Station, Texas

Dear Stuart,

When I was littler, we had the thame problem with my brother Bobby. He felt left out, ethpethially after I won a jacksth conteth at school.

**This is one of me and my brother Bobby. This was when he was trying to find something as good as my mom—Kitty Karry-All.**

So I got Deacon Jonesth to come to our house and that made Bobby better. Maybe you could get Deacon Jonesth to come thee your brother, too.

If you don't have a lot of money, maybe you could thay your brother is dying and Joe Namath will come to your house for free.

**Thindy Brady**

Dear Cindy,
   Is it true that you're dead? And did you have a crush on Mr. French or your Uncle Bill?
   Lisa Gabrielle
   New Castle, Delaware

Dear Lisa,

I'm not sure what you mean, but my thister Marcia once thought her dentist wanted to marry her, but he just wanted a baby-thitter.

**Thindy Brady**

```
Dear Cindy,
  So, am I like your dog or what?
Tiger
```

## Cindy's Best and Worst

**Best doll—Kitty Karry-All.**

**Worst doll—Mrs. Beasley.**

**Best way to get even with your brothers—
    tattle to Mom.**

**Worst way to get even with your brothers—
    tattle to Dad.**

**Best cutest boys—
    Jody Davis and the kid on *Gentle Ben.***

**Least cutest boy—Bobby Brady.**

**Best dad—Mike Brady.**

**Worst dad—Brian Keith.**

**Best servant—Alice.**

**Worst servant—Mr. French.**

**My sister Marcia and me. This is when our brother Greg washed up on the beach with his surfboard. That'sth why we look scared.**

**This is Kitty Karry-All.**

Dear Cindy,
  I have a research report due for third grade, and I thought maybe you could help me with it. It's about Neil Armstrong landing on the moon. Know anything about this?
  Mandy Carter
  West Warwick, Rhode Island

Dear Mandy,

Are you crazy or what? If you thay thomething like that, your teacher will give you a bad grade for sure. Write about how cowsth make milk or thomething neat like that.

## Thindy Brady

Dear Cindy,
    Of all the humans in this weird house, you seem to be the one with a brain. I have written several times now and have gotten no response, other than from your dimwit sister Jan. Do I, like, belong to anyone around here or do you guys think I am just like some kind of lawn ornament no one ever sees?
    Tiger

Dear Cindy,
    I am the youngest of my family and I can't say it's been a good thing exactly.

**Lemonade is a great way to raise funds for your family's taxes.**

You being the youngest, does it ever just
make you, like, want to pull your shirt
up over your chest on national TV?
  D. Barrymore
  New York


Dear D.,

    No, but my maid Alith once lost my Kitty Karry-All's dreth and underpants in the laundry room when she was washing curtains.

### Thindy Brady

Dear Cindy,

  My mom says we have to send my dog
somewhere else to live because he
attacked a girl with her doll on my
street. I say he wouldn't have done it if
the doll's dress hadn't been this bright
red, and it's not my dog's fault the
Danehower girl got eaten. She was a
crummy kickball player, anyway.
  Dakota Williams
  Hot Springs, Arkansas

**Here I am eating a really good isth cream cone.**

Dear Dakota,

Well, first, has your dog eaten anybody before? If not, maybe it *was* the dreth. I just know Kitty Karry-All would never make anybody eat anybody. I hope her doll didn't get eaten, too. My daddy would never take my dog, Tiger, away.

Hey, maybe you could get Joe Namath, the football player, to come to your house and talk to your mom.

**Thindy Brady**

# **Bobby** Tells All

**(How his blond hair turned dark under the strain of growing up a Brady)**

**W**hen I was a kid, like before I could remember anything—like even before my dad and my new mom got married, this kid next door asked me once if he oughta get a turtle. And I kinda had to think, ya know? Like, if it was a whole box turtle or a bowl turtle or if he'd rather have a mouse because his sister would be afraid of it and that would be at least one thing of a guy's that his sister didn't touch.

Then again, I got three crummy sisters I didn't ask for because my dad married my new mom and they still get into my rats and stuff. But all sisters aren't crummy, just when they get into your stuff or don't let you in the bathroom or when the parents make them go camping with you and they bring chicken instead of livin' off the land. My big brothers say that's really bad.

Other than that, sisters are okay.

My mom is okay, too, and so are my dad and my brothers.

If you can say all those people are okay, then your life is probably okay and not crummy.

But never be afraid to keep a picture of your old mom, because if your new mom is really a nice new mom and not like the stepmother in *Cinderella* (my sister's sissy book), then it will be okay to have your old mom around still, even if she's kinda dead.

Also, never go near a cave in Hawaii if you even *think* that Vincent Price guy might be in there.

Here's some of my mail, which I was able to read through with minimal difficulty.

```
Dear Bobby,
  So am I like your dog or what?
  Tiger
```

Dear Bobby,

I've written several times now, and no one in this family (other than Jan) will respond to me. Am I like your dog or what?
    Tiger

Dear Bobby,

I am about your age, I think. My mom and dad let me watch R-rated movies, but they get mad when I look at my older brother's magazines that he hides under his bed. Do you ever have trouble with your folks and what they'll let you watch?
    Tyler
    Ishpeming, Michigan

Hi, Tyler,

Yeah, I kinda know what you mean. My folks say we gotta turn off the TV Sunday nights sometimes because Carol Burnett gets too dirty.

**Bobby Brady**

**Gosh, I hope they don't move in any closer to me.**

Dear Bobby,

My sister was in a bad car wreck and will take months to be okay again. Her husband, if you could call him that, has left her because he doesn't want to deal with her recovery—or their three kids.

The kids' grades are dropping and the oldest wants to quit school. The youngest is your age. She can't work and her disability is hung up in bureaucracy. Please, talk to me.

Claudia
Irvine, California


Dear Claudia,

Well, my mom lost her voice once when she was supposed to sing in church on Christmas, and my sister Cindy asked Santa to bring it back and he did. When it gets near Christmas, maybe you could do that.

Cindy talks real funny and is a girl, too, and Santa still listened to her.

**Bobby Brady**

## My Favorite Foods
### by Bobby Brady

Space Sticks
Razzle gum
Wacky Wafers
Sweet Tarts (the big ones)
Tang
Nestle Quik
Bottle Caps
Sugar Smacks cereal
Ding Dongs and Ho-Hos
Sno Balls
Bosco
Jawbreakers
Circus Peanuts
Sour Apple gum
Tuna and Chee-tos sandwiches
Nutty Buddies and Push-Ups
Pink Things at Six Flags
Pop Rocks
Zero bars
Fizzies
Pixie Sticks

**I don't look as cool as my brothers (my brothers say), but I think I look pretty good here.**

Dear Bobby,
  My dog lives with my dad, and I am only
with my dad every other weekend and some
weekdays when my mom is at her acting
classes. This means I really miss my dog
because I never get to see her.
  I know you never really get to see your
dog, either. Do you miss him?
  K. Marie Phillips
  King of Prussia, PA


Dear Marie,
  Well, I don't see him a lot, but I'm sure he's in the
doghouse we keep in the backyard. Say, why doesn't
your dad just move in with your mom so you can see
your dog?
  Hope this helps,
  **Bobby Brady**

Dear Bobby,
  My parents grounded me for a whole
month just 'cause I took all the heads

off my rottin' sister's Barbie dolls.

I say no fair 'cause I only did it 'cause she bugs me and my friends all the time. And besides, it's not like you can't fix 'em real easy by just poppin' their heads back on. (Well, okay, one's head won't go back on, but the rest are fixed now.)

Anyway, I know you get bugged by your sister Cindy all the time. Have you ever messed up Kitty Karry-All and got in trouble?

What can I do to get off being grounded?

Signed,
Brandon P.
(Grounded in Cincinnati)

Dear Brandon,

Sorry to hear you got grounded. That's really a bummer. Kitty Karry-All got lost once and I kinda got blamed for it for a while.

**My sister Cindy and I in Hawaii. Because we're the same size, we kinda end up staring at each other a lot.**

You're right about sisters buggin' you and stuff, though. Our family went camping once and Dad made us boys go fishing with the girls, who just totally messed up our fishing. Cindy even fell in the water!

Anyway, I think you should get even with your sister another way next time she bugs you and your friends. Pulling on Cindy's pigtails *really* bugged her and it was her word against mine afterward (no messy doll heads lying around).

To get off being grounded, try being extra nice to your parents. You know, offer to wash the Astroturf in your backyard or do the dishes or something.

Good luck,

**Bobby Brady**

---

## Bobby's Guide to How to Deal with Brothers, Sisters, and Parents

1. **If your sister has pigtails and is bugging you, pull them.**

2. **If your sister has a favorite doll and is bugging you, pull its head off.**

3. **If one of your sisters wears a stupid wig, pull it off. Laugh at her with your older brother so you're not the only one Dad hollers at.**

**Being like Sherlock Holmes was really neat.**

4. If your older brother has to go to a birthday party where an ugly girl will bother him, tease him about it a whole lot. (It's only fair 'cause he teases you all the time.)

5. If your older brother's voice changes, tease him about that, too. (It's only fair 'cause he teases you about being a shrimp all the time.)

6. If you need money, just do stuff that bugs your dad while he's trying to get work done, and he'll pay you to go away and leave him alone.

7. If your dad is trying to teach you a lesson about something, just smile and act like you understand. Otherwise, he'll say it again and make you even more confused.

8. Always be nice to Mom, 'cause if you're not, she'll make Dad teach you a lesson.

**This is where we all actually talked and paid attention to Jan.**

Dear Bobby,
    I think the White Power Ranger and
Batman are *totally awesome.* Who are your
favorite super heroes?
    Sincerely,
    Brett Sandhofer
    Hobbs, New Mexico


Dear Brett,

I really like Batman a lot. I watch his show every week. *Da-Da, Da-Da, Da-Da, Da-Da Batman!!!* That song at the beginning and end is so cool. As far as the Lone Ranger goes, I liked his horse Silver more than him.

Sincerely,

**Bobby Brady**

# Extending the Meat Loaf with **Alice**

### (Or, who needs money? Working for the Bradys is its own reward)

**W**ell, first I gotta tell ya, Mr. Brady—oops, sorry, I'm just so darned used to answering to that guy. Anyhow, I may have to leave any minute because before long, I'll probably think I smell my pot roast burning.

I've found—in some, what is it, twenty-some years as a maid now?—that the best way to get along in life is to have a husband—unfortunately, Sam's idea of romance is putting those silver rings on the end of a sausage.

Without a husband, I usually find that a good meat loaf works best for being the happy kind of people the Bradys are.

Also, another key to happiness is a cold-water rinse and plenty of fabric softener to keep the Bradys clean.

Oh, oh, oh, and don't forget, feed the Bradys' dog regularly and stop to feed the Bradys at any hour of the day and that will pretty much keep you at your ol' tippy-top best. But enough about me.

Red is a good color for a big dance at the Elks Hall, but league uniforms are best for bowling. Use powder blue with uniforms only if you spill a lot and have a lot of ol' kitchen mishaps but never seem to get a stain.

If you want a man to marry you, it's probably best to— well, heck, I think I smell the three-bean salad burning. Meanwhile, please feel free to look through some of the letters and my advice.

Dear Alice,

I have been dating this guy for six years. We had a baby a year ago and have lived together for some three. But he will not marry me. I recall that you and your boyfriend have dated for quite some time and he still hasn't come around.

```
Alice, what should I do?
Marsha Pansini
Saint Cloud, Minnesota
```

Well, Marsha,

You know, I know a little girl named Marcia, but it is spelled just a little different.

Well, actually, she's not so little anymore.

But if this man hasn't married you yet, then I wouldn't count on it. Then again, Sam has never popped the question to me, so I wonder if that means . . .

I think I better go now, something smells fishy in the kitchen—or I guess that would be chickeny since it's chicken pot pie I smell burning.

Mr. Brady will be home soon.

**Alice**

```
Dear Alice,
    This is difficult to say, but I gotta
tell you that I have admired you a long,
long time. I frankly don't know how you
```

or Sam will feel about this. It's just
that you seem like such an outgoing woman
and one who isn't afraid to wear a scout
uniform camping or to be athletic or to
make those zany jokes.

God, Alice, you just make me bust a gut.

Could I maybe come and see you just to
meet? I live near you (I think within a
few hundred miles) and my little pickup
truck is still new so it's good to go.
You gotta truck?

I could come on Sunday (softball on
Saturday nights). Hey, maybe you should
try that instead of bowling.

Melissa (you can call me Mel or my
nickname, Cactus Flower)

Indianapolis, Indiana


Hello, Melissa,

Uh, I appreciate your interest in my truck, but I take
the bus.

By the way, Cactus Flower, that's an unusual name,
isn't it? Do you do a lot of gardening?

Oh, I better go, I think I smell the icebox pie burning.

**Alice**

Dear Alice,

Every year here we have this big PGA golf tournament and that's one of the places where my ex-wife goes to pick up guys. That is where she is right now. I think it stinks. I work on weekends, and she leaves my son with her maid when she goes to sports events, which also include Texas Rangers baseball games, to pick up guys. (And that is why she goes, because I know she doesn't know a Will Clark from a living trust.)

Alice, she has a map she and her girlfriends have drawn showing the spots where they can find the Dallas Cowboys drinking. They even know where Troy Aikman gets his suits altered, for Pete's sake.

And to top it all off, her maid stinks. And I'm paying for that maid! You know, if she had a maid like you while she was off on her dalliances, I could stomach my son being there. But no, Faye (that's her maid) is a chain-smoking witch who once dated Jack Ruby (the guy who killed Oswald, if that tells you anything) and doesn't do jack once her lard butt hits that sofa (I bought).

```
    And dear god, Alice, you'll appreciate
this as a cook—her face has higher
viscosity than my Lexus engine and looks
like that white stuff that forms when you
refrigerate juice from the roast.
    Decatur Gilbert
    Fort Worth, Texas
```

Dear Decatur,

Have you ever considered getting together and talking with your ex-wife about this? That works for Mr. Brady, usually, in that he talks it over with his wife, Carol, when one of the kids has acted up.

Hon, it sounds like you have more on your mind than the maid. Would you like to come over and chat in the breakfast nook? I've got a batch of wedding cookies planned for Tuesday, and you could come at 2:30 to beat the after-school rush.

And I'm sure if you can sing or dance, the Bradys would be happy to take you in for a while. Also, tell Faye that maybe she should consider Mr. Clean to really improve herself, dear.

**Alice**

**Well, here's me and Mr. and Mrs. Brady. I guess sometimes this is as close as I'll come to being part of a married couple.**

Dear Alice,
  Haven't you ever wanted to ditch the
Bradys and go to Merry Maids or
something? And does Mr. Brady take care
of your health insurance?
  E. E. Kennedy


Dear E. E.,
  Well, luckily, I never get sick, so health insurance isn't
a problem. I just couldn't work for a big ol' company,
though, because I wouldn't have these six kids hanging
around all the time. Then there's Mrs. Brady, you know, I
need to be helping her understand the dryer controls, oh,
and Mr. Brady needs to have food to smell when he
comes in the door. That man loves to smell food. And
Mrs. Brady gets such a darned kick out of working the
dryer now and then.

  **Alice**

## Alice's Seven Good Ideas for Making Ends Meet on No Salary

1. Wear same powder blue maid's outfit for twenty-odd years.

2. Arrange special meat tradeouts with butcher.

3. Waste not on hair-care products.

4. Go shopping with Mrs. Brady, collect toiletry samples.

5. Geeky nurse shoes last a really long time.

6. Mooch off boyfriend for bowling money.

7. Complain enough about not being married so that your boyfriend will at least get you stuff now and then.

Dear Alice,

I have a hard time getting blood out of my son's bandannas. He is in a group he says is not a gang, but frankly I'm tired

of having to worry about him. I just worry about my job and part of that is the laundry and stains in his bandannas. He says it is vampire blood from a charity haunted house the friends are working on for October. But frankly, it's June and I have my doubts about just what kind of a haunted house could take that long to get ready.
   What do you think?
   Faye Louise
   Denver


Dear Faye,

   It sounds like your son has joined some kind of boys group, but maybe not the Boys Club or Boy Scouts, but something.

   Now, charity is a real nice thing. Why, those Brady kiddos are always in and out of here raising money by being in some kind of variety show. Gee, I think that's great.

   As for the vampire blood, I wouldn't worry too much, as Mr. Brady says, it's just a phase he's going through, like when Bobby, the youngest, believed in vampires for a while.

Funny though, we never had to get a stain out. Say, you don't think these vampires are real, do you? Awww, what am I thinkin'?

Well, hey, good luck, and I'm sure everything will turn out okay.

**Alice**

**Here's where I told Greg that even famous rock and whatchamacallit stars had to clean their rooms.**

Dear Alice,

My mom makes this most retarded salad (she calls it salad) every holiday and stuff. She said she ate it when she was a kid. But the deal is, if a salad could be out of style, this would be. I mean, it's, like, embarrassing because she actually thinks it's, like, good, and she isn't just cooking it to be funny or anything.

It's, aw geez, I forget what you call it, but it's got, like, this lime gelatin junk and cottage cheese and it looks like dog barf, like if the dog ate something besides food—like, you know, a Frisbee or something.

Oh, man, and don't get me started on this other one that's, like, marshmallows and cherry and that frozen whipped cream. That one looks like barf from eatin' a Wham-O toy, too.

Geez, do you make that kind of junk?

And how can I tell her she is gross and way out of touch without hurting her feelings?

Angus
Ogden, Utah

P.S. And can you believe this queer-dog
name she gave me?


Well, Angus,

Now, you seem a little upset about marshmallows.
Mr. and Mrs. Brady say the best thing to do is to eat what
is put in front of you and be darned glad of it. Funny,
none of the Brady kids has any trouble with that marsh-
mallow junk, as you might call it.

Angus, maybe it's none of my business, but is there
something else that's bothering you, like maybe a boy at
school is picking on you? Or you made a bad grade?

Maybe if you came over and had some pound cake and
milk in the breakfast nook, you'd feel a lot better about
things. I'm sure the Bradys wouldn't mind even taking you
in to live for a while, especially if you could sing or dance.

**Alice**

**What a wacky pose! Mr. Brady caught me again with his crazy Kodak Instamatic.**

Dear Alice,
   Have you ever thought of just dumping
the hell out of Sam? I mean, so what if
you get a bunch of free meat. Sounds like
Sam gets his share, too. Man, Alice, I
know he gave you a bowling ball once, but
it ain't like you oughta be waiting
around just to be that guy's ball and
chain.
   You stupid or what?
   Shonriqua
   Alamogordo, New Mexico


Dear Shonriqua,

   My, what a lovely name, Shonriqua. I have never
heard of a name like that, dear. Well, no, I never thought
about splitting up with Sam. I know he'll come around,
and in the meantime, well, it's not like twenty-seven
years is a long time to wait, what with all the extra benefits of dating the butcher. And what with the new
league season coming up at the lanes, and, well, bowling
is only growing in popularity, just like meat. I think I'd
be foolish to . . .

   You know it isn't exactly a gravy train being with that

man. I bought curtains for his apartment, for godsakes—an apartment I don't even live in and never will, for that matter.

I think I'll head over to my neighborhood butcher right now and . . .

Oh, goodness, I left the iron on over my dress for the Kiwanis dance with Sam tonight. You know, he is a member of the chamber of commerce.

**Alice**

Dear Alice,
    I have dated a guy for three years—count 'em, three years. We do everything like we're married except this one little thing—walking down an aisle, and I don't mean at the Piggly Wiggly. How do you deal with Sam in this regard?
    Lorri Ruth
    Hagerstown, Maryland


Dear, dear Lorri,
    I find the way to a man's heart is through his stomach,

and the way to a ring is through a good plate of Polish sausage and sauerkraut or a big plate of Swedish meatballs with extra sauce. Oh, and bread, dear, they love bread. Believe me, the walk to the minister starts with the walk to the checkout counter, if you know what I mean.

Then again, I've been feeding Sam for about three decades now, and twisting my hair like he likes it into

**Mr. Brady got me with his gosh-darned Kodak Instamatic again—and still with no ring on that hand. Then again, it is my *right* hand.**

side knots and letting him call me Helga and, come to think of it, all I've got on my finger is a bunch of cake icing right now.

And I paid darned good money for those lederhosen with the leather . . .

I'll get back to you, Lorri, the kids will be home soon. You know kiddos can make the darnedest messes.

**Alice**

Dear Alice,
My sister dates this real dysfunctional creep. He has a lot of money and the payment on his car phone is probably about the size of my house payment—and I live in a gated community, for heaven's sakes.

She is active in Junior League and volunteers at the country club when they have celebrity golf tournaments. Obviously, you could not ask for a brighter, more well-rounded, giving woman.

He thinks money makes him, and he

doesn't have to lift a finger to be a
good man. I'm concerned for my sister and
would appreciate any of your wonderful
wisdom that I could pass on to her.
    Zemetrius Utlanta Johnson
    Vicksburg, Mississippi


Hello, Zemetrius,

Well, it sounds like you have a problem. Hey, speaking
of fingers, any ideas from you about getting Sam to put a
ring on mine?

Best of luck,

Alice

P.S. My, Zemetrius certainly is an interesting name.
I've never heard a name like that before.

Dear Alice,

    Just had to write you back. Man, are
you whacko or what? Geez, you're so
obsessed with that sack of lard butcher
guy, no wonder that he doesn't want to
marry you. I don't give a whit about this

weirdo thing you have going with Sam. Did you hear me ask about my sister?

Man, wake up and smell the fast food, lady, this is the 1990s.

Zemetrius Johnson,
in Mississippi

Dear Alice,

I continue to try to search for a more mature look for myself. I enclosed a picture and wonder what you would think if I did my hair like yours. Frankly, I'm not sure how you get the bangs rolled up around your forehead like you do.

No one seems to like my hair, however I do it. I even wonder if my husband does, sometimes.

Hillary C.
Out East

Dear, dear Hillary,

Well, looking at this picture here, don't take offense, but that isn't your natural hair color, is it, honey? Dear, maybe folks would like your hair better if you just picked one hairstyle and stuck with it.

Unless your husband prefers blondes, why not let your own color shine through? My hair is just a mess, honey. I don't know why you'd want yours to be like mine.

Say, would you like my green bean and Durkee onion casserole recipe? That'll sure get your husband's attention. The Bradys and my boyfriend Sam really love it. They say the way to a man's heart is through his stomach and the way to the preacher is through the taste buds. I just hope he stops by the jeweler first.

Come to think of it, I've been cooking for that man for years and nothing, absolutely nothing. I had a chance with the postman once and just tossed that out the window like dirty dishwater.

I do and do and do for that man, and I paid good money for that French maid's outfit and . . .

Honey, shave it bald and dump the rat, they ain't worth it.

Well, Mr. Brady is waiting on rolls.

**Alice**

**Here I am, hands all tied up in sweeper cord. Oh, the hands always make me think of fingers, which make me think of rings—aaaeeew!**

## Alice's Ten Tips for Being Real Good Domestic Help

1. Leave kitchen area only to deliver one-liner in den—or to supervise kids in Hawaii.

2. Always exit the room with a scene-closing non sequitur.

3. Never make a pass at Mr. Brady, even though that perm is pretty happening.

4. Do your best, despite the kitchen missing one wall.

5. Work twenty-plus years with apparently no pay.

6. Borrow Schultzy's duds to save Bradys uniform money.

7. Cook a lot but don't eat.

8. Wipe hands on apron a lot to save paper towels.

9. Make meat loaf in twenty-pound portions.

10. Scurry.

**They always love it when I use these special mushrooms.**

Dear Alice,
   My mom is so busy. We don't have a maid, like you, to cook for us. All my mom ever does is throw chicken fingers, which she gets one hundred at a time from Sam's, in the oven. I used to like chicken fingers, but not every night. I'd sure like at least some buffalo wings or something.
   Ruby Westfall
   Arlington Heights, Illinois

Dear Ruby,

How long has your mother been feeding you like this? I can't get the Brady kiddos to eat the liver, much less the fingers. Come to think of it, dear, chickens don't have fingers or rings, do they? Oops, 'scuse me, the subject of fingers always reminds me of rings, like the one I don't have on mine.

Anyway, sweetheart, this really isn't good nutrition. Sam doesn't even sell chicken fingers and he's cheap enough to even sell *beaks*. It sounds like this friend of yours, Sam, must have a big farm. Could you go stay with Sam for a while?

And, dear, I can't reach Sam right now to ask him about the buffalo wings you mentioned, but is that a name for the shoulder blade area of the buffalo? And aren't they extinct?

Sweetie, I think you better come over and talk to Mr. Brady about this.

They would probably even let you live here a while. There seems to be no end to the room in this crazy-with-a-tilted-K household, and if you can sing and dance, they might adopt you.

**Alice**

# Chewing the Fat with **Sam** the Butcher

**(Or, how to avoid matrimony at all costs)**

**S**ome people don't think that I, as a butcher, give stuff a whole lot of thought. But I went to school, and I was smart enough to find a little gal who bowls and cleans up real good when we go out. All I gotta do is keep her in the meat. And, friend, that's what I suggest you do, too. Just keep your friends, particularly those special little friends you wanna keep around, in da meat.

And furdermore, you'd be a fool to go to the grocery store. Heck, with them big stores, the butcher is a trained professional.

As for women, I guess I already told ya to keep 'em in

the meat, but to all you boys out there, I wouldn't rec-
ommend dating any less than twenty- to thirty-odd years
before you marry. Remember, the women make good little curtain makers and cooks, but then you gotta keep
'em around all the time. No time for cards, if you know
what I mean.

A gal will hate the smell of a cigar, too. Remember that
when you're thinkin' this might be the little gal you want
to spend the rest of your life with. If it were me, I'd just
keep giving her rump roast to keep her happy. Yeah,
everything pretty much does come down to meat, if you

**They say dancing is a really "groovy" way to let off steam.
Even the people in the street seem envious of how much fun
the Bradys have, although I don't get it.**

know what I mean. Let me fill you in some more by refer-
ring to the ol' mailbag here.

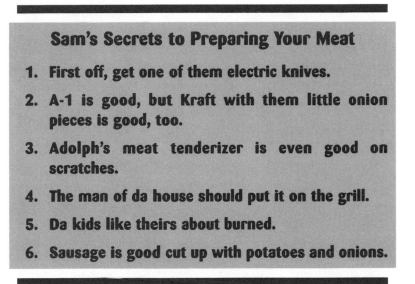

### Sam's Secrets to Preparing Your Meat

1. **First off, get one of them electric knives.**

2. **A-1 is good, but Kraft with them little onion pieces is good, too.**

3. **Adolph's meat tenderizer is even good on scratches.**

4. **The man of da house should put it on the grill.**

5. **Da kids like theirs about burned.**

6. **Sausage is good cut up with potatoes and onions.**

Greetings, Sam,
   I'm writing you with a rather ticklish
question. You see, I'm a rather finicky
man when it comes to dating. In fact, my
pals Norm, Woody, and Sam say I'm a bit
too finicky. I, of course, prefer to

think of myself as a man of refined
tastes with extremely high standards
where womankind are concerned.

At any rate, you seem to have made
quite the catch there with Alice, the
maid, and I was kind of wondering how a
man like me might procure a similarly
loving, devoted woman. Also like you, I'd
rather not be weighed down by matrimonial
concerns, if you get my meaning.

Best regards,

Cliff C.

Boston, Massachusetts

P.S. Like you, I'm a practical man of
modest means who's been working on the
same job (as a postman) for several
years. I should also note that I live
with my mother, or I mean to say, I take
care of her and her home. So, a maid-type
woman would be perfect for me.

Dear Cliff,

I am a man who feels that at this stage in my butcher
career, I need to stay loose, with marriage kinda weighing
a guy down heavier than one of those beanbag chairs full
of ground beef I send home with Alice.

Now, Cliff, if you think you might have an interest in Alice, I gotta warn ya, she wants one of dem wedding rings and frankly, I don't know how much longer I can keep her on a string without the ring, if you know what I mean.

Yet as I always say, "Why buy the cow when you can get da milk for free?" or "Why go for da side of beef when they's handin' out free Little Smokies every day at the meat counter?"

So, if you think you can handle this, maybe for a few tradeouts on some meat products and even some of dem summer sausages, you might want to start dating my little lady.

Alice might even be okay on livin' with your mom—or takin' care of her.

Just a thought.

**Sam**

Dear Sam,
  You're a man who really knows how to handle his meat and his woman. That's why I'm writing you.

```
  You see, I work at the meat counter in
our town's grocery store and have been
dating this girl in produce for almost
two years. Her name is Lacey, and she's a
great girl who really knows her
vegetables. Plus, we get along really
well. I like her a lot, and she's all
I'd ever want in a woman. She thinks it's
time we got married, and I'm thinking of
proposing. But, gosh, it's a big step,
and I'm just not sure. What should I do?
  Jonathan Spelich
  Franklin, Vermont
```

Dear Jonathan,

Sounds like you two go together like meat and potatoes! But, hey, that's no reason to go rushin' down the marriage aisle. Heck, you never know—tomorrow some girl at the deli counter, in the bakery, or in the checkout line could catch your eye, and then where would you be? If you're not sure, then take your time. There could be some great buns in the bakery waiting just for you.

Best of luck,

**Sam**

**This is my girlfriend Alice—that was one of those times she mentioned something about an empty ring finger.**

Dear Sam,

Are you in love with Alice or what? Son, I am eighty-two years young, and I can tell you that is one fine woman you have there with the kind of spunk they didn't have in my day.

I have been happily married for some fifty-three years, and my wife has stood by me, brought food to my table, and been pretty darn much the runner of this household.

The fact that she is domestic help isn't bothering you, I hope.

Why don't you marry the girl, Sam?

Mr. Schwepps

Worcester, Massachusetts

Dear Mr. Schwepps,

Well, to tell you the truth, sir, frankly I liked her better as Schultzy.

**Sam**

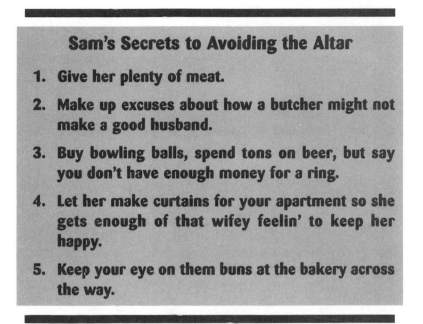

## Sam's Secrets to Avoiding the Altar

1. Give her plenty of meat.

2. Make up excuses about how a butcher might not make a good husband.

3. Buy bowling balls, spend tons on beer, but say you don't have enough money for a ring.

4. Let her make curtains for your apartment so she gets enough of that wifey feelin' to keep her happy.

5. Keep your eye on them buns at the bakery across the way.

Dear Sam,
  What is your favorite kind of meat? And do you carry soft-shell crab?
  Shawanda
  Rome, New York

**Well, here's Alice, again, and me dressed like we're going to a wedding. No, not ours, pal.**

Well, Shawanda, Say, that's a different name, Shawanda. What kind of name is that?

Well, I've never met a piece of meat I didn't like. And I wanna say right now, we got no crabs in this place what-soever. No crabs, lady. That is a lady name, right?

What kinda lady would ask about stuff like that? I bet you bowl with men, don't ya?

**Sam**

Dear Sam,
    I have been dating a nice girl for
seven years now. As you know ladies are
prone to do, date 'em more than six years
or so and they expect a ring on their
finger, if you know what I mean. I recall
that you and Alice have dated for twenty-
some years without you ever having to
take the plunge.
    So Sam, how do you keep 'em on a string
without a ring?
    Rick K.
    In the Heart of Big D


Ricky Boy,

I know what you mean, buddy. Why buy the cow when you can get the milk for free, huh, big guy? The secret is in the bull. Take it from a man who knows how to keep a woman happy without havin' to be lassoed by Clara-bell—if you want to keep the rump roast comin', you gotta give up some real good pork chops and about twenty pounds of ground round a week.

Lamb chops is good now and then.

And if you really think you might be serious about this

little gal, then don't wait for a minute to give her one of them little pink, girlie bowlin' balls that are kinda shiny like the back of a fish aquarium. Now, I'm not sayin' you gotta go so far as to join a league with her or nothin', 'cause you don't want her too much into it. But more than anything, just remember from the Butcher here, a pound of sausage ever' now and then is worth a thousand rocks.

**This was the time the Brady kids listened to Jan.**

Them's just my words, in case you thought I was a poet or somethin'.

**Sam**

Say, Sam,
   Like, I was wondering, what do you think of those Bradys?
   Like, on *Bewitched* they drank. On *I Love Lucy* they smoked. On all these other shows they have sex kinda. Isn't it just kinda weird that all they ever do is eat at that breakfast table and Mike never comes in soused or sits there cooling his forehead with his martini glass?
   I bet Carol even wears full-throttle cotton underwear—no thongs, no nothin'.
   Carl
   Stationed in Germany


Dear Carl,
   Lighten up, buddy, it's a TV family on a TV show. Thank God, or else I woulda had to marry Alice by now.

**Sam**

# Brady Episodes We Might Never See

1. **"Spittin' Image":** Inexplicably, Carol spits and grabs crotch after being bestowed the honor of singing the National Anthem at a Dodgers game. Bedlam ensues as Mike and the kids make a zany race for the exits, and Marcia frets about the incident affecting teen model career. Wes Parker appears as himself.

2. **"The Mentor":** Mike Brady takes young architect I. M. Pei under his wing, and the kids go on a zany caper to procure a spot as the lead singing act at Mike and I. M.'s opening at the Guggenheim. Davy Jones guest stars as himself.

3. **"Bobby Gone Bad":** The family is all abuzz as Bobby gets mixed up in a bad crowd and unknowingly participates in a drive-by shooting. Martin Short guest stars as the principal.

4. **"Hair Today, Gone Tomorrow":** Siblings unite as Marcia seeks to win the approval of Sinead O'Connor by waiting at the stage door and shaving her head. A madcap dash to the studio ensues as five other Bradys rush to save Marcia's teen model career. Tommy Smothers guest stars as O'Connor.

5. **"The Subject Was Sherliquas":** The Bradys adopt a mixed-race child, and the whole crew goes on a whirlwind shopping spree at Sears in search of ethnic duds. Mike and Alice get out the encyclopedia in a madcap hunt for ethnic names and customs, only to find out the child has since been placed with a more suitable family.

6. **"The Middle Ground":** Cindy waits at the hotel bar for Chicago Bulls basketball star Dennis Rodman and persuades him to visit her sister Jan. Rodman visits

the Brady home and reassures Jan that it's okay to be different, and he suggests a red wig. Guest star Jimmy Walker keeps the laughs coming as the Bulls' assistant coach.

7. **"The Affair":** Mike succumbs to the affections of cosmetics mogul Beebe Gallini, but the deal is off after Greg spots the two at the local pizza parlor. There's no end to the comedy as kids learn sometimes it's okay to tattle even on your dad, and Mike and Carol work things out in family counseling. Bill Clinton guest stars as the group therapist.

8. **"Will the Real Mrs. Brady Try to Stand Up?":** Macramé flies as Mike gives Carol black eyes in a domestic dispute over a hug-rug project gone bad, and the kids secretly get a singing act together in the garage to pay for Dad's bail. Slappy White guest stars as the inmate.

9. **"I Like Mike":** After viewing Mike's prowess as a neighborhood association leader, friends urge him to seek office. The political fur flies as Mike runs for

Congress but is drummed out of the race for his out-spoken views on abortion, handgun regulation, pro-tectionism, and a wacky trade war with France. Rush Limbaugh guest stars as the madcap political advisor.

10. **"Mike's New Job":** Mike loses his job at the firm after designing a geodesic dome home for the new city hall. The Brady dad begins selling Amway, and piggy banks unite to buy Dad's cleaning products and save the house. Carol applies for food stamps as Mike begins drinking and there is no end to the frolic as Alice breaks the tension with an impromptu soup line. Sonny Bono guest stars as a congressman.

Author Jennifer Briggs has written for *Sports Illustrated, USA Today,* the *Fort Worth Star-Telegram,* and the *Dallas Observer.* She was included in the 1993 edition of *The Best American Sportswriting.* A lifelong fan of the Bradys who still loves using Marcia's condiment formulas on her hair, Briggs also performs standup comedy and lives in Dallas with a dog slightly more visible, loud, and stinky than Tiger.